All About Looting: Exploring Looting as a Form of Protesting

Table of Content

Introduction

This Book takes an in-depth look at looting. In chapter 1 of the book, you will be introduced to looting as a concept. Furthermore, this chapter will cover examples of what constitutes looting, when looting is most likely to occur, and factors that may increase the likelihood of looting.

In chapter 2, you will learn more about what looters do. This includes why people loot, the specific actions that people can take when they loot, and why looters may decide to target certain places over other options, such as for political reasons or to garner attention for their cause.

Moving into chapter 3, the various consequences for looting are explored. While it may not be intuitive, looters can be charged with a wide variety of other charges, such as assault, trespassing, theft, and burglary. Thus, this book explores some of these legal charges and their potential consequences, which range from misdemeanors to felonies, which varying fines and consequences. Financial considerations in defending someone against a looting charge, such as legal fees and court costs are also explored in this section.

As we switch gears into chapter 4, the semantic and legal differences between stealing and looting are unearthed. How are these two terms different? You will be able to see some examples of what is considered stealing versus looting to help illustrate these seemingly similar concepts. Very important in the distinction between the two terms is the role of context, which is also covered.

Turning to chapter 5, readers will get a better sense of reasons why looting may or may not be considered a form of protesting.

 Chapter 6 covers which businesses are most likely to be targeted for looting. Although many looters prefer to go for stores that have valuable items, larger stores are typically able to rebound much more quickly from the damage than are smaller stores. This means that smaller businesses that do experience looting bear the brunt of the impact. Looting can happen anywhere, but it is far more common in cities than it is in suburban or rural areas of the country.

Chapter 7 explores how often people loot. The frequency with which people loot as well as their motives are not always known. More research needs to be done to better understand this dynamic.

Chapter 8 looks into the concept of arrest rates after looting. This chapter introduces the reader to the idea that arrests can occur immediately, at the moment, when police are well prepared for riots and looting. However, arrests can also occur later, using media coverage of events and after police look through video surveillance of the area where the looting occurred. Recent numbers on arrests related to looting and protests are discussed in this section.

As the book shifts into chapter 9, an in-depth examination of how police prepare for and respond to looters and protesters are presented. When preparing for these situations, police tend to prepare by making announcements to the public so they are aware of areas that will be closed down. They also tend to call in extra support, both in terms of additional police officers and in terms of key stakeholders who know both viewpoints. Police may wish to issue curfews as one tactic. When dressing for these events, police use special equipment known as protective riot gear. They may also implement traffic directions, first aid stations, and think through ways they will disperse the crowd if needed. The last part of the section explores responding to looting and protesters.

Switching to chapter 10, a look at where looting is most frequent comes into focus. This book briefly explores which cities in the United States have experienced the most looting. Additionally, countries in the world that have experienced high rates of looting are also covered.

Chapter 11 provides some historical context for how looting began. Additionally, this section of the book also discusses ways in which looting has changed over the years.

Black Lives Matters Movement, is the main focus of chapter 12. If you have not already heard of this movement, you will be introduced to it for the first time here. This relatively young organization has been a driving force in the call for social equality. It has been a major player in calling for, organizing, and holding peaceful protests to demonstrate the unequal treatment of Blacks in today's society. This chapter covers when the Black Lives Matter Movement was founded, who founded it, and what the beliefs of the movement are. Additionally, the global actions of the movement are discussed and financial and non-financial ways of supporting the Black Lives Matter cause are presented for anyone reading who would like to lend their support.

Chapter 13 introduces readers to another relatively new organization with a similar aim to Black Lives Matter. The Color of Change fights for social equality using an online platform. Information is presented about current campaigns, how to donate, and the mission of the Color of Change Organization. Additionally, information is provided for those who would wish to become involved with this organization.

Chapter 14 provides a pivot into looking into the history of police brutality against Blacks and the data that supports this phenomenon, which has now been more aptly named as part of a public health crisis. Cases that grabbed headlines and media attention for police brutality against Blacks are discussed. Next, measures taken to prevent police brutality and the impact of such measures are reviewed. Looking towards the future, this section will also cover additional measures that could be implemented to protect Blacks from police brutality in the future.

Chapter 15 focuses on the recurrent killing of unarmed Black people, often by police officers who use too much force. These have now become an apparent trend across American cities where police officers fail to utilize de-escalation techniques when arresting Blacks compared to Whites. Blacks are much more likely to be injured during an arrest than Whites are. To illustrate the point of how frequently and unnecessary the killing of unarmed Black people is in America, this book highlights the deaths of seven different unarmed Black people.

The first two cases of George Floyd and Eric Gardner have striking similarities. Both are Black men, albeit in two different American cities, who allegedly committed minor offenses and were killed by police before they ever got to the police station. Floyd was being arrested for allegedly using a counterfeit $20 bill while Garner was allegedly selling single cigarettes out of a pack. During the arrest, officers used restraint positions that caused both of them to lose consciousness, in combination due to the restraint position and excessive force combined with pre-existing health conditions.

We also review the cases of Freddie Gray and Breonna Taylor, who both died far too young. In Taylor's case, she never knew the police were coming and was shot dead while asleep. A bright student and hard worker, she worked as a medical technician and her only fault was being Black and dating someone who the police suspected was selling drugs. Police never announced themselves, and thinking that intruders were coming into the house, Taylor's boyfriend fired a shot before officers shot Taylor eight times. It is thought she did not die until the eighth shot hit her.

The next two examples of Natasha McKenna and Tanisha Anderson also have sickeningly surprising similarities. Both of these women were Black and in their late thirties. Likewise, both women had documented histories of mental illness which were known to police. Both women were killed when police tried to arrest them while they were experiencing exacerbations of their mental illness. In McKenna's case, her family called in hopes of summoning an ambulance to transport her to the hospital. Instead, police came and she lost consciousness while the excessive force was exerted upon her by police. She arrived at the hospital and despite attempts to resuscitate her, she lost consciousness. Anderson was actually in prison and died while a specially trained six-man team, who was aware of her mental health symptoms, used a taser on her four times before she lost consciousness and never regained it. Both women were also mothers and left behind young daughters at the time of their deaths.

The final case involves 17-year-old Antwon Rose. He died from gunshot wounds inflicted upon him by a police officer, who was never sentenced for his role in the shooting. All he did was run from a car that was pulled over by police.

Chapter 16 reviews looting laws. It answers the question of whether looting is considered a crime and gives readers insight into how state laws differ in terms of their reactions to looting. It also touches upon a unique topic that can be overlooked when it comes to looting, which is looting that occurs during a designated state of emergencies of other crises. These laws are specifically important to understand as looters will be prosecuted more strictly during times of declared emergencies than during peaceful times. This chapter also explores possible punishments for acts related to looting and what you can do for yourself or a friend if one of you is ever accused of looting. Given the life-changing ramifications of a looting charge, it is very important to educate yourself about what steps you should take if you find yourself in that position.

Chapter 17 provides suggestions of ways that you can defend your home or business from looting. Given recent looting events, it has become clear to many people that waiting for police support that may not come is not a viable option. Suggestions for defending your home from looting include obtaining a guard dog, keeping outdoors areas very well lit, using heavy-duty locks, and investing in plexiglass instead of glass.

To defend your business from looting, many concrete suggestions are provided. These include temporary options such as hiring additional security during times of unrest to simple options such as keeping pepper spray on hand. Using security cameras and adding steel bars are also covered in this section. Only one state allows for the use of deadly force to protect property but only under certain circumstances, which are also summarized in the portion of the book.

Chapter 18 covers the seemingly confusing concept of people destroying their neighbors in an act of protest. This surprises people who might imagine that protesters and looters only target neighborhoods where they do not live. Reasons for this behavior are discussed in this section as well as whether the act is intentional or unintentional.

Chapter 19 provides a worldwide view of looting. This section looks into what issues have incited looting around the world. To start this portion of the book, the most recent protests, namely the George Floyd protests, are covered in the United States and across the globe. In this chapter, looting is discussed as it related to Hurricane Katrina, the Mexico Gas Prices Hike, and Greece's famous archeological looting that has occurred for centuries. Hopefully, this should allow readers to understand some of the many different reasons and causes that looting can occur. It also discusses examples of looting such as the Boston Tea Party, the London Riots of 2011, and others.

Chapter 20 explores how looters see their actions. Do they view looting as a problem or do they feel that it is justified due to some slight, such as decades of abuse by law enforcement personnel?

Chapter 21 meanwhile, looks at the role that journalists have played about the looting. It discusses how they balance the need to accurately report what is happening although their coverage can sometimes result in additional looting. Likewise, it discusses how the coverage they provide can be used to apprehend those who engage in looting. Lastly, it provides an overview of injuries that journalists have sustained during looting events.

When it comes to looting many people wonder how the damage is fixed and who is responsible Thus, Chapter 22 gives the reader insight into who is responsible for covering the cost of fixing the damages stemming from protesting and looting. In many cases, this is done through insurance policies, but in some cases, it could be up to the individual homeowner or business owner.

Chapter 23 discusses the important need for Whites to join in advocacy efforts. More so than just joining in, it discusses how White people can examine their privilege, listen to communities who are experiencing oppression, and then take action to become a strong ally. This involves exploring your talents and abilities to see how you can best advocate reducing systemic oppression and discrimination.

Chapter 24 demonstrates how high-level officials can lack awareness and understanding of the causes and reasons for looting. It can also show how the responses of high-level officials can incite additional looting. This chapter reviews how major world leaders have reacted to instances of protests and looting. Included in this section is the recent incendiary tweet from President Trump. It also looks at how the less restrictive response of Mayor Bowser in Washington, D.C. as well as a harsher response to protesters which was evidenced in Tiananmen Square in 1989 in China.

Chapter 25 illustrates how social media provides a variety of ways to track down looters. Aside from the options of Instagram, eBay, Craigslist, Facebook, and Television Footage. If the police have specific leads, they are also able to track social emails or messages that the suspect sent to his or her friends. In today's society which relies heavily on technology, police continually develop more refined methods to help apprehend those who engage in looting.

Chapter 26 describes how social media plays a major role in finding how people sell stolen goods as well as how police can intervene to recover stolen items. However, there is much more to the story of looting than just social media. This section discusses what looters can do with stolen goods and how police can recover them.

Chapter 27 illustrates the freedom of expression. In general, most protests are safe and do not turn into looting frenzies. Many safety precautions will help you plan how to safely attend protests and exercise your first amendment right. However, even if you are not the one causing disruptions or violence know that police can respond to others present who are. Thus, you will want to plan a getaway strategy and follow safety tips.

Chapter 1: What is Looting?

Definition of looting

When you hear the word 'looting' you may think back to the history textbook you read when you heard about pirates plundering and looting from boats. Outside of that context, what does looting mean? In modern days, looting refers to the act of stealing something from someone else. The items that are stolen generally are valuable. It is also important to note that looting generally occurs during times of civil unrest, such as war, protests, or natural disasters. Looters typically obtain items they steal by using some type of violence or force.

Examples that constitute looting

Now that the definition of looting has been established, it is possible to cover examples of looting to clarify the meaning of the word. Looting has been used by people and countries all over the world for a variety of reasons. In the 1500s, Spanish Conquistadors targeted countries in South America for looting. Namely, they wanted the gold from Peru and Mexico, which resulted in many Spanish troops entering the aforementioned countries and looting gold and other high-value items from the Aztecs. During Hitler's reign, the Nazi party looted valuable cultural artifacts, such as priceless art, from people who practiced Jewish faith, as well as other minority groups who opposed the Nazi Party. In the United States, looting has occurred after major disasters, such as Hurricane Katrina, which caused people to break into stores and homes to obtain food, shelter, water, and other supplies to survive in the aftermath of the massive New Orleans' storm. In 2015, Baltimore erupted with protests, which included looting, after the senseless death of Freddie Gray by the hands of police. Currently, protests are occurring across many cities in the United States to protest the death of George Floyd. These protests have occurred in many major cities, such as Washington, D.C., Los Angeles, Seattle, Minneapolis, Detroit, and Atlanta. While the majority of protesters are peaceful and nonviolent, smaller groups of protesters have incited arson and looting to garner attention for their cause. This led to break-ins at luxury stores, fast-food restaurants, and individual homes. These are just a few examples of what looting constitutes and there are many other times throughout history when citizens of the world have engaged in looting.

Situations when looting is likely to occur

One aspect that is unique to looting is that it is likely to happen in certain situations. It is very common for looting to occur after natural disasters. Many people are more tolerant of looting after natural disasters as many people are desperate for food, water, shelter, clothing, and other necessities. Recent flooding in Texas and Louisiana have shown that when people lose access to their own homes and property, looting occurs. This may mean breaking into grocery stores to obtain necessities or obtaining needed items from other damaged or abandoned homes. Similar looting has occurred after hurricanes, tornados, earthquakes, and other weather-related events.

Another situation that is likely to be a precursor to looting is civil unrest and protests. For example, the assassination of Martin Luther King, Jr. led to looting, arson, riots, and other acts of vandalism as a protest against the unjustified death of a civil rights activist. Looting has also been known to occur during times of war. Another situation that can lead to looting simple opportunity. One of the most famous cases of opportunity looting occurred in New York in 1977. This year, a blackout occurred during which time groups of men looted stores and broke the glass on the front of major New York City stores. This led to hundreds of millions of dollars in damage.

Factors that lead to the likelihood of looting

There are a variety of factors that are linked with the increased likelihood of looting. One of those factors is uncertainty. In times of uncertainty people's fears are activated and there is less certainty about what will occur. One example is the COVID-19 pandemic, when people felt uncertain and began looting supplies from hospitals, such as hand sanitizer and face masks. This also holds after floods and other natural disasters, when there is uncertainty around how long it will take to be rescued or to obtain necessary supplies. Another factor that increases the likelihood of anger is the level of anger around political ideology or civil unrest. For example, there was outrage on behalf of the Black community after many Black men and women were killed unjustly in the United States by police brutality. Both uncertainty and anger can increase the likelihood of looting.

Where is looting most likely to occur

Looting is most common in large cities during times of crisis. However, it can occur in smaller cities and rural areas, especially after a natural disaster. Looting tends to occur when there is an opportunity and to promote political or social ideology. One of the most common times looting occurs, aside from after natural disasters, is during protests. During protests, individuals involved typically are trying to further their cause. While most protesters tend to be uninvolved in looting, some groups take advantage of the opportunity with distracted police and start looting from businesses or private homes. Looting is also common in times of war or civil unrest.

Chapter 2: What Do Looters Do?

What causes people to loot?

People loot for many different reasons. The first reason that people loot is due to necessity. As previously discussed, in times of crisis such as after a flood or hurricane, there may be a large number of people who are displaced and unable to access resources that they need to survive. Desperate times lead people who would not otherwise consider looting to take supplies to ensure that they with their families can survive.

The second cause of looting is to go along with a group. Many people begin protests with the idea that they will not be involved in anything illegal. However, they may be convinced by others, or simply caught up in the excitement of the moment, to engage in groupthink and join in looting behaviors. With police distracted with large numbers of protesters, it becomes easier for those who want to loot and to have the opportunity to engage in it. Looters may loot to make a statement, such as looting stores that do not support their ideologies or to loot those who are making statements or who have policies against their cause.

What actions do looters take?

Looters engage in specific actions, such as vandalizing property and stealing. In terms of vandalization, looters may break the windows of various storefronts to gain entry into the building, which can cause substantial damage. Looters may also damage other aspects of the business, such as damaging goods, spray painting, or breaking items inside of the store or home. Another action that looters take is stealing items that do not belong to the looter. The stealing can occur from either a private residence or a place of business. After a natural disaster, people may end up stealing from their neighbors or neighborhood stores to get the necessary supplies. During protests, this may involve stealing items, such as televisions during the 1977 blackouts or luxury items from stores during the George Floyd protests.

Why do looters target certain places?

For those who go somewhere with the intention of looting, several areas go into why they target certain places? As previously mentioned, the opportunity is an essential component of looting. If there is no opportunity to loot, looting will not occur. An opportunity will not arise if there is a high police presence and if there is a high level of security. Thus, looting occurs when the police are distracted or unable to get to areas, due to blockades or protests. Preventative measures, such as security guards and well-lit areas can help prevent looting from occurring.

Certain areas are also targeted for looting due to political reasons. This may be because the actual location that gets looted has ideologies that people want change, so they attempt to use scare tactics to force change. For example, there were large protests when Donald J. Trump was elected president. And protests were observed throughout his presidency to demonstrate a lack of support for his policies and statements.

Looting can also occur as a mechanism to garner support for certain social causes. One example of this can be seen through animal cruelty prevention efforts. Companies that manufacture or sell cosmetics that have been tested on animals have been targeted by looters. In some cases, looters have stolen test animals and set them free, vandalized property, and left messages in graffiti. They hope to draw attention to the need to stop animal testing.

Lastly, some areas are targeted because they have items that someone else needs. After tornados or hurricanes that result in extensive damage to cities or communities, people may loot food, gasoline, clean drinking water, clothing, or other supplies from wherever they can get it. Looting occurred extensively after Hurricane Katrina, from homes in New Orleans, grocery stores, other businesses, and even from other survivors at The Super Dome.

What do looters do with the merchandise they took?

You may wonder what looters do with all of the goods they took. There are several main things that people do with looted goods. The first is to use or consume the items themselves, which is most common after natural disasters. For the looting of luxury items, the looters may try to earn a profit off of the stolen goods. Thus, they may try to pawn the items at a pawn shop or try to sell the items themselves on Craigslist or eBay. In other cases, the looted merchandise may be destroyed as a form of protesting. This could take the form of setting fire to the merchandise, breaking the merchandise or otherwise damaging it beyond repair. In more rare cases, the merchandise may be donated to different organizations.

Chapter 3: What is a Looting Charge?

The legal definition of a looting charge

Looting laws typically vary by state and country. In the United States, for example, the government sometimes imposes additional penalties during times of crisis or emergency. In general, looting is comprised of other changes, such as burglary or theft. Additional charges that may apply include vandalism, assault, trespassing, and others depending on the context in which the looting occurred.

Legal consequences of a looting charge

While engaging in looting behavior may seem like no big deal at the moment, it can have damaging, and long-term consequences. In many cases, the accused will need to hire a lawyer that comes at a significant personal financial cost to defend themselves against the looting charge. However, the charges for looting are typically comprised of different charges. That is to say, there is no looting charge by itself. Rather, you are likely to be charged with one or more of the offenses below:

Theft Charge

A charge of theft means you have been charged with taking property that belonged to someone else. It also has a component of intentionality, meaning that you meant to take something that belonged to someone else and that it was not an accident. In minor theft cases, the value of the items stolen typically range between $500 to $1,000 and can involve minimal jail time or minor fines. Theft of low-value items is typically classified as a misdemeanor. However, there is also grand felony theft which involves the taking of more valuable items. The exact amount is determined by state law. This type of charge comes with more jail time and additional fines, compared with petty theft. It is noteworthy to point out that there are major differences in thefts that are classified as a misdemeanor and thefts that are classified as a felony; felony charges typically require serving at least one year of jail time.

You might be wondering how misdemeanor and felony charges are assigned to looters. Aside from the consideration of the value of the stolen items, sentencing considerations also factor in whether there was violence involved in the theft as well as the person's history of previous thefts or other crimes. Although theft can seem like a light charge, it is important to differentiate what type of theft you are being charged with as the consequences can drastically differ.

Burglary Charge:

Burglary involves stealing something from someone else and it is considered a statutory offense. This means that someone enters another person's home, car, business, or other property to take something that does not belong to them. Additional charges may be added to the burglary charge, such as breaking or vandalism. When considering sentencing, some factors impact the length and severity of the sentence. These can include whether a weapon was used to commit the crime, whether there was the intent, the presence or absence of other people at the time of the burglary, and whether the burglar was using substances at the time he or she committed the crime.

Punishment for burglary varies by state and by whether the accused is being charged with first- or second-degree burglary. The first-degree burglary occurs when someone else is present at the site of the break-in, and often carries penalties ranging from about five to thirty years in prison. On the other hand, a second-degree burglary occurs when no one else is present during the break-in, so punishments are less severe. Typically, punishments for second-degree burglary range from just a couple of years to fifteen years in jail.

Vandalism Charge:

A charge of vandalism involves the purposeful damage, destruction, or wrecking of another person's property. One example of something that could be charged as vandalism is using graffiti to cover the walls of buildings. In many states, the value of a destroyed property plays a role in sentencing. For example, in New Jersey, if the charge was for a property that costs less than $500, the individual would be charged with something called disorderly person offense. However, if the value of the property is more than $2,000, a fine of up to $10,000 and a jail sentence of three to five years could be imposed. The exact punishments will vary state by state. Many states also have special rules for the destruction of certain types of properties, such as gravesites, utilities, and research facilities.

Felony Charges

Many of the looting charges can be charged at the state level, while others can escalate to the federal level. It is very important to know that during the States of Emergency, both states and the federal government have the power to impose restrictions on citizens to protect public safety. Typically, any crimes committed during States of Emergency are prosecuted as felony charges whenever possible.

Arson

The charge of arson is meted out when looters intentionally set fire to a property that belongs to someone else. One aspect that is unique about arson is that set something on fire, even if the item or building is not destroyed, is enough to be charged. Many states treat arson as a felony charge, which can include 15 to 25 years of prison time. However, some states have lower levels of punishment for arson, such as misdemeanor offenses.

Assault

An assault charge most often occurs after someone physically attacks another person. However, it can also include the planning of an intentional assault that was not carried out. In general, there are three different levels of assault that a looter can be charged with. The first type, known as a simple assault, occurs when another person pretends to have a weapon, applies force, or blocks someone while trying to cause harm. An assault that is carried out with a weapon, or the second type of assault, carries stiffer penalties. The most severe type of assault is aggravated assault, in which the victim of the attack is very seriously harmed, disfigured, or even sustains life-threatening injuries. The penalties range from misdemeanor offenses to up to 25 years in jail.

Trespassing

Trespassing is one of the most common offenses that protesters and looters encounter. Trespassing occurs when someone does not adhere to posted signage requiring someone else to stay off of their property. Trespassing must be purposeful; meaning that a hiker who loses his way and wanders on someone else's property is not held responsible. However, someone who purposefully enters a closed park or beach where a "no trespassing" sign is visible, can be charged with this offense.

Rioting

Rioting occurs when violence occurs during a protest. Rioting can involve simply planning or organizing a riot, assisting someone who helped in carrying out the violence during a riot, or being involved in the riot. Specific rioting laws vary from state to state. Rioting during protests can endanger the lives of other peaceful protesters as well as police. As such, it is taken seriously and can be charged as a federal offense.

Other Charges

Aside from the charges described above, many other charges may apply to looters and protesters. These can include disturbing the peace, homicide if someone is killed during the looting, and many others. Additionally, looters can be charged with more than one crime at a time. For example, someone who breaks into a business to loot may be charged with breaking, vandalism, and theft. Given the complexity of charges that looters can receive, it is important to think about the financial consequences of looting.

Financial Consequences of Looting

Paying for legal representation

Legal representation in the United States is extremely costly. Simply retaining a lawyer can cost anywhere from a couple of thousand dollars to $100,000. This is the amount you will need to deposit for the lawyer to agree to take your case on. Your actual cost will vary by the number of hours the lawyer has to spend on your case and you will be billed hourly. Many lawyers charge several hundred per hour. They charge for all phone calls, meetings, research, and time spent in court to represent you on your case. In addition to the actual lawyer's fee, there are sometimes additional fees for legal aids or assistants who help with the case. Additional fees may also be applied for photocopies of documents you need, driving expenses, and court filing fees.

The cost of legal representation varies widely based on experience and location. If you need to hire a lawyer to defend yourself about looting, you should ask what they charge per hour and how much their retainer costs. Additionally, you should ask how many hours they anticipate your case would take so you have a general sense of the financial commitment you are making. Some lawyers will work a minority of cases pro bono, meaning that no compensation is required, while other lawyers will be willing to accept a lower hourly rate. If you are experiencing financial need, ask your lawyer if he or she is willing to consider a sliding scale or reduce fee arrangement for your case.

Fines

In addition to fees related to legal representation, looters who have charges brought against them can often expect to pay fines. Fines for looting can vary, even costing tens of thousands of dollars towards the higher end of the scale. In addition to fines for the actual looting, those accused may be charged with court costs or fees.

Jail

Anyone who is facing a looting charge should make certain that they secure qualified, legal aid as soon as possible once they are arrested. This is because heavy jail time can be imposed, such as 10 to 25 years in prison. The sentencing phase will depend on the severity of the looting, the value of items destroyed, and the context in which the looting occurred. Anyone who is jailed, even if only for one to two years, faces the heavy burden of loss of income, loss of freedoms, as well as other inconveniences. Therefore, you will want to find a lawyer who has experience representing previous clients successfully for looting charges. A good lawyer will help you decrease the amount of time you are facing or win your case without jail time.

What should I do if I am charged with looting?

If you are accused of looting, you may feel scared, confused, or angry. It can be hard to know what to do in the heat of the moment. If you are charged with looting, the first thing you should do is try to stay calm so that you can think clearly. Being offering any information to the police about what happened, ask for your lawyer. If you do not have one, ask a family member or friend to call a lawyer on your behalf to represent you.

Once you have legal representation set up, it is important, to be honest with your lawyer. Think through what happened. Be truthful when giving a step by step recall about the events that led to your charge. You will only hurt yourself and your case if you lie to your lawyer (e.g., saying you were not there) and then later recant if additional information is found that does not substantiate your claim (e.g., a videotape recording of you being in the area). The prosecutor could use this against you to discredit your story.

In addition to being truthful, adhere to facts. Try to avoid adding in your own or your friends' interpretations of what happened. Just stick to facts. Ask your lawyer what they recommend. Your lawyer will likely advise you of your chances of having charges withdrawn or thrown out if that is a possibility. Make sure to bring up any mitigating factors.

In addition to obtaining legal counsel and being honest with them, you will want to present yourself well in court. Practice preparing for answering questions from the prosecutor with short, succinct answers. Do not volunteer any extra details. Simply answer the question you were asked.

After sentencing, make sure to comply with any fines or sentencing requirements. Let your lawyer guide you through the process. Make sure you are informed and ask thoughtful questions.

Chapter 4: What is the Difference between Looting and Stealing?

Difference between stealing and looting

Have you ever what the difference is between stealing and looting? You have likely heard these terms over and over again, especially given recent events. However, when you sit down and think about stealing and looting you may feel confused about what the difference is between the two words. The confusion you are feeling is merited because stealing and looting are very similar. There is a minor difference between the two words as a trick to help you remember the difference.

Stealing is something that can occur anytime. It is when someone takes something from another person without permission. For example, if you are walking down the street on your way to work and someone grabs your purse, then that person just committed the act of stealing your purse. Steal has other meanings as well. For example, if you find a really good bargain on an item at the grocery store or while out shopping, you might hear someone say that is such a steal. In that sense of the word, it means you have found a great price or a bargain. Another meaning of the word steal is to sneak away quietly. For example, you might say that two dinner guests like to steal away to see the night stars and take a break from the company of the other guests.

Looting is very closely associated with the word plundering. It often means taking someone else's property, but usually occurs during certain periods. Namely, looting is most likely to occur during times of civil unrest, during times of war, during natural disasters, or during protests. Looting also generally refers to a large amount of property being taken, but the same is not true for stealing. For example, throughout history, pirates have looted and plundered from other boats passing by. Another example would be looting that occurred after the unjustified killing of Freddie Gray to draw attention to the excessive use of police brutality against the African American population.

Thus, the main difference between stealing and looting is relatively minor. The best way to remember the difference between the two words is to think of "loot" and "lawless." Looting is likely to occur during times of lawlessness while stealing can happen any day or at any time.

Examples of stealing and looting

To better help you understand the concepts of stealing and looting, this book will provide more examples in case the small nuances are not yet clear. If during a protest, small groups of people begin to smash storefronts and take electronics, clothing, or other items of value from inside the store, that would be considered looting. Likewise, if a hurricane hits and people who are unable to be rescued begin taking things from their neighbors' houses, that would also be considered looting. On the other hand, if during times of peace someone enters your home and takes your silverware, that would be considered stealing. Another example of stealing would be if someone goes into a store and walks out with a blouse without paying for it.

Importance of context in differentiating looting and stealing

It is so important to understand the context in which the act occurred, as that helps determine whether the act should be considered looting or stealing. For the word looting to be used, there must be some type of special circumstance. Special circumstances could include war, social unrest, protesting, or riots. Stealing occurs in the absence of special circumstances.

Legal standards for prosecuting stealing vs. looting

The legal standards for prosecuting acts of looting and stealing vary by state. The penalties can range from misdemeanor crimes to felonies. Fines varying from a couple hundred to thousands of dollars can be imposed as well as jail time ranging up to 25 years. Each state has different severity levels to help determine what the punishment will be.

Chapter 5: Is Looting a Form of Protest?

Reasons why looting may be viewed as a form of protest

When citizens want to raise the alarm of social or political injustices, protesting has been a well-documented form of doing so. Some people think that looting adds to their cause. They believe that looting brings additional attention to their message. Likewise, it brings into the equation people who may have otherwise stayed out of the protest (e.g., business owners, police, victims, etc.). In certain circumstances, looters target certain businesses to protest their business methods or practices. This can be readily seen in research facilities, labs, and pharmaceutical companies that test on animals. Animal rights activists may try to loot these locations by freeing the animals held captive or by taking other supplies that are necessary for daily operations. Looting often makes headlines in newspapers and makes the evening news, so more people are aware of the cause of the group behind the looting. Other times looting occurs impulsively and without forethought. In this way, looting may or may not be a form of protest, depending upon the circumstances and the motivations behind the looters.

Reasons why looting is not a form of protesting

On the other hand, looting may not be a form of protesting for several reasons. As previously mentioned, looting may occur impulsively and without forethought. In that sense, looting does nothing in terms of assisting with a protest plan. Likewise, looting can cause significant damage and have major repercussions throughout the community, state, or country where it occurs. If the majority of people do not agree with the cause, it is unlikely that the looting will change their minds. It is also important to note that while peacefully protesting something is legal in the United States and guaranteed under the first amendment of the constitution, looting is illegal. In that sense, looting is typically frowned upon and looters can be charged with a variety of legal charges while peaceful protesters cannot be charged. Thus, in general, looting is different from protesting.

Chapter 6: Which Businesses are Most Frequently Looted by Looters

When it comes to looting, you might be wondering whether all businesses are equally prone to looting or whether certain ones are more likely to be looted. The most popular targets for looters are businesses that carry expensive products. However, businesses that stay silent or that are opposed to the views of protesters are also at risk of being looted.

With the recent George Floyd protests, the businesses that are the most likely to be hurt by the looting include smaller businesses. The George Floyd protests came at a time when many parts of the United States were under stay at home orders due to the coronavirus pandemic. As part of that pandemic, small businesses across the country that were deemed non-essential were already hurting from being shut for so long. The looting related to the protests added a whole other complication to the recovery efforts of small businesses in the United States.

Many small businesses say that between the global pandemic and the looting stemming from the protests, they will not be able to survive and plan to shut their doors. Thus, while smaller businesses may be targeted less often when they do experience looting they are more likely to be significantly impacted. In many cases, these are small family-owned stores. Sometimes owners do not have coverage that will pay for the damage to the store or for the merchandise that was damaged and now cannot be sold.

Larger stores such as Macy's, Target, Walmart, and other major chains tend to have more resources and can recover more quickly.

Additionally, other sites can continue making money while one site is under repair. Smaller shops are the ones who bear the brunt of the impact.

It is important to understand that looting can happen anywhere and at any time. However, it is most likely in times of civil unrest. It is typically more common in urban areas than it is in rural areas. Since looting can happen anywhere, it is important to take some of the preventative measures discussed in a previous chapter to protect your home and business to the extent possible.

Chapter 7: How Frequently Do People Loot?

Looting is most likely to occur by low-income and working-class people. These are the people who tend to need resources the most and who are most likely to risk the consequences of being caught while looting. In some cases, though looters have no choice.

In the days after Hurricane Katrina hit, some people designated as looters were simply people who were trying to survive. With everything washed away, they went to the stores looking for diapers, clothes, food, and other necessary items. Looting based on survival needs is different from other types of looting. This survival looting can occur anywhere there is an area that is majorly impacted by a natural event, such as an earthquake, flood, or hurricane.

Looting during protests is much more sporadic. While many people choose to join protests to peacefully demonstrate for one of their ideals, things can quickly shift when one or more small groups of people branch off and begin looting. When it comes to looting, the motives behind the looting as well as the number of times a person loots is not always easy to discern. It appears that some people engage in looting once based on opportunity while others engage in looting more frequently to gain attention.

Chapter 8: How Many People Are Arrested After Looting?

One question that people frequently have about looting relates to the number of people who are arrested for looting. Some people naturally assume that looters get away with their acts because the police are overwhelmed. However, other people tend to think that looters are held accountable. Which is more accurate? The answer is that it depends on many factors.

In recent months, George Floyd and Black Lives Matter protests have shed some light on how many people are arrested. While exact numbers specifically for looters are unavailable, in early June 2020 Chicago reported arresting over 3,000 citizens for charges related to civil unrest, which included acts of looting, particularly near the Southside of Chicago. Yet, similar protests in Long Beach, California during early June led to only about 28 arrests. Thus, there are vast differences in the number of people arrested for the same acts. What causes these differences?

One main cause of the difference in arrest rates is how overwhelmed the police department is during the looting. Police departments prioritize safety, so there are times when they will not be able to access the area to arrest people for looting. Likewise, when police departments are overwhelmed there are fewer officers available to handle large crowds. So, does that mean that looters get away with their goods without any recourse? Not necessarily! During the protests of early June 2020, cities such as Los Angeles combined the skills of their police departments with FBI assistance to look through video recordings of lootings. Thus, even if looters are not arrested during or right after the act, there is the possibility that video footage of the looting is available from the business they looted from or from video recordings from the surrounding area. In addition to using video recording, police have begun to utilize Facebook and other social media platforms to make arrests related to looting.

Another factor is that the police department across the United States have differing views on the number of protests and unrest that they will tolerate. As one example, the mayor of Washington, D.C. has been relatively sympathetic to peaceful protesters but denounce the destruction of property. Other cities have taken a stronger stance against protests and implement additional resources to curb looting. Thus, the number of arrests related to looting vary widely by city, the number of available police, and other factors.

Chapter 9: How does Police Prepare and Respond to Looting and Protesting

Preparing for Looting

While sometimes police are reactive and have to respond at the moment, often when it comes to looting and protesting there is time to develop guidelines. When police departments think through ways to prepare for planned protests, what do they think about? Below are some of the ways that police can prepare for protests.

Announcements to the Public

One way that police can pre-plan for protests and possible looting is to alert the public. This allows people who are not involved in the protests to avoid the area. It also makes clear to protesters that there will be a police presence.

Extra Support

When police are made aware of protests, they call in extra support. This may involve collaborating with key stakeholders, including the people who are organizing the rally. In addition to the people or organizations who are protesting, the police may also reach out to groups with opposing viewpoints who may also participate. Additional key stakeholders, such as those who live in the community and owners of businesses may also be contacted.

In addition to reaching out to the above stakeholders for information for and against the protest, the police are likely to enlist additional police staff members to help with the actual event. This may include specialized teams, K-9 units, or police who use horses. All of these measures are typically taken as precautionary measures depending on the anticipated size of the crowd.

Curfew

In cities where violence, arson, or looting is expected, the mayor of the city may impose a curfew. Police can also make this recommendation to a mayor to help abate looting. When a curfew is implemented, individuals are still rightfully allowed to peacefully protest up until the time that the curfew begins. All citizens must be at home during the curfew hours. Cities such as Washington, D.C., and Los Angeles, CA implemented curfews during the George Floyd protests. Baltimore, MD implemented curfews during the Treyvon Martin trial.

Typically, the curfews mandate that individuals stay inside during certain hours. These hours often fall between sunset and sunrise. In addition to issuing curfews to help control riots and looting, they can also be used to help police plan after natural disasters and during times of public health crises. Curfews can be applied to everyone or only to minors without adult supervision.

Riot Gear

When it comes to equipment, police want to plan as best they can to keep everyone safe. During riots and protests, this often means preparing for what could occur if a peaceful protest turns violent. Thus, even if only a peaceful protest is anticipated, you will likely see police stationed in riot gear. Riot gear involves the use of a large riot shield to protect their bodies and to use it as a barrier against protesters if needed. Additionally, it involves wearing a riot control suite that offers more protection than traditional police uniforms. Often, you will notice that officers at protests wear a special kind of helmet that has a face shield protecting their eyes and nose.

In some cases, you may wonder what the strange-looking black mask they are wearing is for. Police can recommend or use tactical gas masks for all or some officers at riots. One nonlethal method of controlling crowds that get disruptive is to use tear gas to disperse the crowd. The gas masks protect the officers from the gas while affecting the people who do not have gas masks. Additional protective equipment for police and riot gear is determined by local authorities.

Traffic Blockages

A unique responsibility of the police is making sure that traffic is not blocked and can still flow, while also blocking off paths that the protesters may be using. This balancing act is typically done upfront and alerts vehicles of off-limits areas. If the path of the protesters' changes during the march, the police must decide whether to block more areas to vehicular traffic or whether to reroute protesters to their planned route.

In certain protests, there has been tension between protesters and police-related to traffic flow. One of these instances occurred during the 2020 Atlanta protests when a large group of protesters blocked a very busy interstate, thereby rending traffic to a standstill. The police were attempting to use de-escalation tactics to avoid loss of life.

First Aid

When preparing for riots, police need to think about how they will respond to any injuries that arise. This could be injuries sustained by police officers or protesters. It may involve having an ambulance and other first responders on the scene. Alternatively, it could mean having access to basic first aid supplies at a designated first aid station. In areas where large riots or protests are expected, there may be a need for more than one first aid station to serve the number of people who are anticipated.

Managing the Potential Need to Disperse Protesters

Police are required to allow peaceful demonstrations to take place, as citizens are entitled to their first amendment rights. Yet, when demonstrations turn confrontational, police are required to maintain safety. In general, they should use the least amount of force possible. As a first step, you may hear them announce to disperse. If you want to remain safe, it is in your best interest to disperse when requested to do so by the police.

If rowdy crowds do not disperse, police have the option of using additional means to protect the safety of the public. This can include tear gas, which inflames the nose, eyes, and throat. It makes it difficult to see and breathe, so people want to get out of the area. Besides, to tear gas, the police may use rubber bullets. These bullets are specialized in that they do not enter a person's body. However, that does not mean that they do not cause damage. There have been some reports of rubber bullets blinding people, causing severe bruising, and being responsible for other painful injuries. Other options may include using pepper spray or tasers.

Responding to Looting and Protesters

The decision of how to respond to protesters and looting varies widely across the United States. As previously mentioned, police can use a variety of tactics to quell unruly crowds during protests, such as pepper spray, tear gas, and rubber bullets. When it comes to looting, the police use many interventions to respond and gather information. One of the first things they want to know is where the looting is occurring. This allows them to put additional police officers nearby or to have police officers in that area keep an eye out for any suspicious behavior.

In some cases, police have collaborations with organizers of the protest and can figure out who is doing the looting. This can help them separate those responsible for damage from those people who are simply peacefully protesting their point of view on an issue. If police know who did the looting, they can quickly and easily target those responsible while keeping innocent people safe. They generally may inquire about what caused the person or persons to loot.

If those responsible for looting are not known, police still want to act quickly as a failure to respond could lead to additional looting and damage. Thus, police tend to try to contain the area by guiding crowds to another location or through the use of a crowd dispersion technique. They will attempt to keep the area guarded until the damage can be repaired.

Perhaps one of the best tools that the police have about looting is media coverage. Media coverage can help turn the public opinion against the looters who are causing expensive damages. Likewise, they can ask for the public help in finding those responsible for the damage. When possible, police also attempt to look through video coverage, either through the media, police body cameras, or video surveillance of the area, to identify those responsibly. If they can identify those involved in the looting at a later time, looters can face prosecution for their actions then. Police also have the discretion to make immediate arrests if they are in a position and have the manpower to do so. This tends to immediately quell other incidents of looting.

Some of the reaction is dependent upon the circumstances. If the looting occurs after a natural disaster and first responders are trying to save lives, they will be more dependent upon the public and video surveillance to help with the looting. However, if the looting occurs during pre-planned protests which already have a large police presence, the police may be ready and equipped to make immediate arrests at the time that they occur.

Chapter 10: Where is Looting Most Frequent?

Which states in the United States have the most looting?

When it comes to looting, you might wonder where it is the most prevalent. Are certain cities or states more prone to looting than others? Looting does indeed tend to occur in cities more frequently than other areas. Among the cities in the United States that experience the most frequent incidences of looting are some of the major cities that you might expect. These include New York City, Los Angeles, Washington, D.C, and Chicago.

However, certain instances can cause major riots in other areas of the United States. For example, there have been major protests, looting, and riots in Minneapolis where George Floyd was killed. Hurricane Harvey and Hurricane Katrina render many parts of the cities destroyed, so looters began taking what they could. These instances happen due to unplanned weather events, but can also result in major financial costs in other pockets of the United States when victims of looting have to replace belongings.

Which countries in the world have the most looting?

Looting is nothing new and has occurred frequently throughout history. The United States is one of the countries where looting has been highly prevalent. Stemming back to the time when the first explorers to what is now the United States began taking land and belongings from American Indians and claiming it as their own. Looting occurs even today as the George Floyd and Black Lives Matter protests sometimes turn to violence.

Spain is another country that has frequently been looted. Spain was invaded by Britain in 1719, and later by Georgia and Portugal. Under the dictatorship of Francisco Franco, looting from citizens who dissented occurred. Spain was also responsible for looting in another part of the world, namely Peru and the surrounding areas during its quest for gold.

After Germany failed to win World War I, it became the victim of mass looting by other countries, such as Great Britain and France.

Other major countries that have been looted frequently include Greece for its ancient artifacts and Israel also for its historic gems.

Chapter 11: When Looting Began and How it Has Evolved Through the Years

It is thought that looting generally started with individuals who decided to plunder goods from other people. Throughout history, that sometimes has evolved into more than one person joining forces to take property that does not belong to them from other people or organizations for some ideological or political purpose. This has been going on for so long that it is challenging to pinpoint exactly when it first started.

Some countries, such as Greece, have been targeted for a long time for looting due to their exquisite antiquities. Other countries, such as those in North and South American likely began experiencing looting when Spanish Conquerors and other first explorers began pillaging their lands. In America, Native Americans have had their land and property looted since colonization.

Early tactics tended to rely more on force and were less regulated than looting is today. In today's society, many countries have sign international agreements that ban looting during times of war. This is why reports of U.S. soldiers stealing Iraqi archeology and looting other antiquities from Kuwait, Syria, and other countries have been taken very seriously.

In the United States, there are different types of looting. The first kind, looting based on a need to survive, often occurs after natural disasters. When people are unable to get help and when first responders are unable to get in, people become desperate and need to take food or other essential items to survive. These are often people who would not loot under other circumstances. However, there have also been reports of looters during times of crisis who take things that are not needed for survival, in order to profit from it or for their benefit. The second kind of looting is looked upon less favorably.

Outside of times of natural disasters, some protesters have turned to looting to draw attention to their cause. They hope that increased media attention will provide more sympathetic support for the political or ideological view. Other people loot because they get caught up in the moment or who simply take advantage of the opportunity to try to turn a profit. The reasons for looting are varied.

What has evolved the most over the years in terms of looting is laws related to looting. In the United States, these laws vary by state and often depend on the number of goods stolen. Stiff penalties for looting can be applied if the perpetrator is caught, and can vary from misdemeanors to felonies. In addition, additional charges can be applied in the United States for each additional crime that occurs related to the looting. For example, someone who broke into a business to loot could also be charged with breaking.

One additional change throughout history is that individual owners and police have become savvier about preventing and responding to looting. For their part, business owners have invested in upgraded technology to try to catch looters in the act and to protect their livelihood. Police, on the other hand, have enhanced how they locate and prosecute those accused of looting, such as using social media and television coverage to track down and identify suspects.

Chapter 12: Black Lives Matter

History of Black Lives Matter

When Formed

The Black Lives Matter movement is relatively new. It was found only seven years ago in the summer of 2013. Since being founded seven years ago, the movement has garnered media attention and successfully gained major support for their cause.

Who founded Black Lives Matter?

The Black Lives Matter movement was co-founded by three women. The first co-founder, Patrisse Khan-Cullors, is a Los Angeles based organizer and artist. She is a former Fulbright Scholar and is an award-winning author. Opal Tometi identifies as Nigerian-American and is based in New York. She has a background in advocacy and communication and she also works as a writer and organizer. The third co-founder is Alicia Garza who is located in Oakland, California. Alicia has worked as a public speaker, writer, and organizer with an emphasis on equality for domestic workers. All three co-founders came together to help combat racism against African Americans in the United States.

Beliefs of Black Lives Matter

The Black Lives Matter movement began with the hope to end anti-Black racism as well as to draw attention to the violence sanctioned by police forces against Black people. The Black Lives Matter movement was able to forge bonds with African Americans and allies all over the United States who held similar beliefs. Black Lives Matter has organized protests to demonstrate the collective power of many voices, particularly after the unjustified killing of Trayvon Martin. The organization is inclusive of transgender individuals and other historically oppressed people.

Global Actions with which Black Lives Matter is involved

Black Lives Matters has partnered with major celebrities, communications experts, legal gurus, and major humanitarian organizations in order to effect change in the causes they believe in. In 2019 alone, they have spearheaded six major global initiatives, including protests and advocacy work for the release of 21 Savage, a rapper who was detained by immigration officials in the United States. In 2018, they gathered at the border between the United States and Mexico to demand just and humane treatment of asylum seekers and immigrants coming to the United States in hopes of a better future. This came at a time when the Trump Administration began tightening restrictions against immigrants and when immigrants who were captured in the United States were being held in temporary housing sites for longer than is legally allowed. Additionally, children were being separated from their parents. Thus, activists at the border were urgently needed to bring attention to the injustice that was occurring at the hands of the United States government.

Supporting Black Lives Matter

Are you interested in lending support to Black Lives Matter? With so many people joining in the movement to combat racism there is no better time than now to support Black Lives Matter! There are many ways that you can help out.

The first way is to make a financial donation. If you are in a position to do so, consider donating money to support the work of Black Lives Matter. If you go to the Black Lives Matter homepage online, there are options to donate $25, $200, $250, or $1,000. There is also a blank box where you can enter a customized amount of any amount you wish. Every little bit helps, so whether you can make a $5, $50, or $500 donation your gift will go a long way in helping to end white supremacy.

If you are unable to donate, you can also get involved by signing a petition online to support the groups' work. There are a couple of petitions for which Black Lives Matter is currently seeking additional support. The first is to advocate for the release of data related to race and coronavirus. The second petition, also related to the coronavirus, seeks more from the government response to the pandemic. You can add your name to either petition through their online website.

Want even more ways to help? At Black Lives Matter, there is an online shop. You can choose and order a gift for a loved one or splurge on apparel for yourself. The items in the store all follow the black, yellow, and white color scheme of the website. There are t-shirts, long-sleeve shirts, sweatshirts, hats, pins, and even masks with the Black Lives Matter logo.

Other ways of helping are by reporting disinformation related to Black Lives Matter on their website. You can also sign up to join the global movement and receive information on advocacy efforts. In order to sign up for updates or the newsletter, you will need to supply for first name, last name, email address, and zip code. With so many options to join this amazing movement, you can consider which method you would like to use to support Black Lives Matter and their ongoing movement for equality.

Chapter 13: "Color of Change" Organization

What is the Color of Change organization?

The Color of Change Organization has nearly two million members and is dedicated to racial justice using an online platform. Among their goals are to decriminalize being poor, halt the expansion of prisons, and creating fair and equitable sentencing guidelines. The President of Color of Change is Rashad Robinson and its Vice President is Arisha Hatch. They lead a large team of staff dedicated to joint goals of creating racial equality and enlisting partners to support them in this endeavor.

What campaigns have the Color of Change run?

Currently, the Color of Change has a number of campaigns dedicated to criminal justice reform. One of their main ones is to defund the New York Police Department while another calls for holding Detroit police accountable for using excessive force on protesters. Other initiatives are aimed at keeping families in touch during the pandemic when one family member is in prison.

Can I get involved with the Color of Change organization?

Yes, there are several ways to become involved with this unique organization from the comfort of your own home. You can first head to this website (https://act.colorofchange.org/signup/signup/) and sign up to receive emails from the organization when they need support. You can also go to the Featured Campaigns and sign up for any of the petitions that you agree with. In addition to the ones mentioned above, there is also a current petition for Breanna Taylor. Using the Contact, Us portion of the website, you can also email the organization to ask about additional volunteer opportunities.

How can I donate to the Color of Change organization?

In addition to donating your time for the cause, you can also make a financial donation if you so choose. Donating to this worthy cause is easy when you click on the Donate button on the website. Buttons are ranging from donations as low as $10 to as high as $1,000. You can also opt to type in your amount into the empty box and set your donation amount. You can donate your birthday to this organization on social media or otherwise fundraise as well.

Chapter 14: Police Brutality Against Black People

History of police brutality against Black people

The United States has a long and sad history of brutality against Black people. In recent years, the impact of systemic racism in police departments and the unjust use of force, typically by white officers against Black folks, have been thrust into the spotlight. This has come about due to some tragic instances where young Black men and women, often unarmed or nonthreatening, have been killed by police officers who are using excessive force. In many of these cases, it has been successfully argued that such force would not have been used against someone who was White.

For more than four hundred years, police departments have acted with excessive brutality against Blacks citizens compared to White citizens. This has led many Black communities to fear for their lives and the lives of their children. Police patrolling Blacks dates back to when slavery was still legally allowed. Even after slavery was abolished, police have continued to display implicit bias, prejudice, and/or hatred towards Blacks. For example, when the Ku Klux Klan was established in the South, it fought to wreak havoc on Black communities by killing and tormenting Blacks in their homes, schools, and communities. They destroyed property, set fires, and killed Black people in hateful ways, such as through the use of lynching. Sadly, some of these Ku Klux Klan members were police officers who hid in anonymity under white robes.

During the Civil Rights protests, when Blacks were fighting to be treated as equal to Whites, many peaceful protests occurred in major cities throughout the United States. The police used excessive force during these peaceful protests, such as using high powered water hoses, arresting people, and using dogs to break up the protests.

Also, in the 1960s, in Oakland California, a group known as the Black Panther Party was created with one of its main goals being to stop police brutality. Unfortunately, the story of police brutality continued into the 60s, 70s, and even remains today. The most recent examples of police brutality against Blacks involve Rayshard Brooks and George Floyd. Rayshard Brooks was running away from the police when he was fatally wounded in the back. The police officers who shot him failed to render aid after the shooting and had several other options to stop Rayshard instead of shooting him. An investigation is currently being conducted into the actions of the police officers involved in this shooting.

George Floyd was a Black man who was also killed by police brutality. For more than eight minutes, he begged the arresting officer to remove his knee from George Floyd's neck saying that he was unable to breathe. George Floyd ultimately died after being unable to breathe and his death was ruled a homicide. There was a total of four police officers involved, none of whom intervened and who prevented bystanders from helping George Floyd. All four officers involved were fired from the Minneapolis police department and are awaiting trial on various murder charges.

The death of George Floyd kicked off a renewed call to action to hold police officers accountable for the use of excessive force against Blacks. Likewise, in recent years, the media has increasingly portrayed police brutality aimed at Blacks through movies such as *The Hate U Give*. Popular books depicting police brutality have also been written over the past several years, including *When Police Kill* by Franklin Zimring, and Sun Yung Shin's book called *A Good Time for the Truth: Race in Minnesota.*

Data demonstrating Blacks at higher risk of police brutality than Whites

In the United States, Whites and Asians are the least likely to be victims of police brutality. African Americans are the most likely to be killed by police brutality, followed by Pacific Islanders. Out of the more than 1,000 people who have been killed by police while unarmed, more than 33% of those were Black. Other studies suggest that Blacks are two to three times more likely to be killed at the hands of police officers than their White counterparts. This has caused an outcry that can be heard around the world and has even incited calls for defunding the police. Major research institutes, such as The Pew Charitable Trusts, some states, and counties in the United States have furthered the cause for equality for Blacks by declaring racism in a public health crisis. Major cities, such as Boston, Minneapolis, and Dallas are among the leaders in citing the health risks of being Black.

Famous cases of police brutality against Blacks

When it comes to apprehending and arresting citizens for suspected crimes, police officers tend to have an abundance of tools in their arsenal. This may include tasers, mace, physical force, guns, and other mechanisms through which they can arrest someone. In the next section of this book, you will get an in-depth look at the surprisingly frequent killing of unarmed Black people.

There have tragically been so many famous cases of police brutality against Blacks, that the cases you are about to read do not even begin to cover the scope of this nation-wide problem. One well-known case was the case of 44-years-old Eric Harris who was killed in 2015. Robert Bates, the arresting officer, claims that he accidentally shot Eric Harris when he mixed up his real gun with his stun gun. Harris was restrained and not armed at the time of his untimely death. Bates was later punished with only four years in prison and was released early for good behavior.

In the case of Michael Brown, there would be no justice for his family. Michael Brown was with his friend Dorian Johnson when they were stopped by Darren Wilson who was a police officer. It is alleged that Wilson began insulting and threatening Brown, which resulted in Brown and his friend running off. After a chase, the officer shot Brown excessively, a total of six times. The statements of Johnson and Wilson contradicted each other in some areas and ultimately no charges were brought against the officer for Brown's killing.

Measures Taken to prevent police brutality against Blacks

Given the increase in police brutality, in conjunction with renewed advocacy efforts for equal treatment by police regardless of color, many preventative measures have been implemented. Intending to hold police accountable, many police departments have reviewed their training guidelines and have offered additional training to current police officers in an attempt to lower the use of excessive police brutality against Blacks.

Starting sometime around 2015, many police departments introduced the use of body cameras. These cameras are equipped with both video and audio feeds for the most part, while others only have video. These were introduced as a way to corroborate what police say by having visual and or auditory evidence of what actions the police officer took when he or she was trying to apprehend a suspect, provide evidence of the actions or statements of the accused, and for training and review purposes. Although body cameras have helped alleviate the problem of excessive force, they are not foolproof. Not all departments require the use of body cameras, meaning that there are some arrests where no video footage is available. Additionally, the video may freeze or experience technological problems during an arrest. Likewise, the video is not able to capture every angle, so there are still portions of a stop or arrest that will not be able to be viewed. In terms of audio, there are major problems when there is excessive environmental noise, such as when an office is near a busy highway or a bustling airport. If the suspect is far away, the audio recording may not capture everything the suspect says.

Another attempt that has been aimed at reducing the excessive use of force is the addition of diversity training into the police departments. However, there is a strong argument that these pieces of training do not go far enough to prevent the use of excessive force or to reduce discrimination. Likewise, many of these pieces of training fail to teach de-escalation skills to officers, so they end up relying more on force than other techniques particularly when someone is resisting arrest.

Impact of prevention measures

Body cameras have played a significant role in holding officers who used excessive force accountable. The majority of officers who were charged for killing someone they were apprehending was made based on the admission of video evidence. Likewise, the didactic training has helped to some extent but are by no means a cure-all for the problem.

Although the use of body cameras and training may help to some extent, they fall short of solving the systemic, nationwide problem of racism and excessive use of force by police against Blacks. What else can be done? There has been an abundance of research on preventative techniques that could be implemented to curb the use of force, which will be discussed in the next section.

What else can be done to prevent police brutality against Blacks?

For decades, there have been several policy suggestions to help curb the use of excessive force. The 2020s have brought a renewed interest in reviewing and analyzing policies that guide policing. Policing task forces have put off several viable options that can be easily implemented.

One of the most important ones is the use of body cameras and to allow cell phone footage of police arrests. This demands that police give suspects choices is how and when their video footage is used, including turning the camera off if they choose. Likewise, this measure would prevent police from requiring that individuals turn off their cell phones.

Police have long relied on a theory called Broken Windows Policing. This theory suggests that when there are signs of a minor crime, such as a broken window, there are likely more serious problems. This policy has led to more frequent policing efforts in low-income communities and communities where Blacks and other minorities tend to live. For example, minor offenses such as jaywalking, loitering, someone experiencing acute symptoms of a mental health problem and acting strange, or drinking alcohol on the sidewalk has led to citizens being killed by police. Instead of focusing on minor offenses, policies suggest creating equitable policing efforts that rely less on community income or color.

Another solution that has been proposed involves having more community representation in police forces. Currently, more than 66% of police officers are White. This solution suggests that police forces be more representative in terms of demographics with the communities that they will serve. This may involve changes needed to how the recruitment of new police officers occurs.

A third policy suggestion that has been put forth is to create more equitable contracts for police, who currently enjoy major protections under union contracts. These protections can make it challenging to conduct reviews of alleged misconduct. As part of this, there is also a push for more clarity in officers who have been accused of using excessive force and methods via which those records could be made available to other departments or interested parties.

Another solution, which also aims to include the community, is to involve community members is the oversight of the police force. The way the police force currently works is that when an allegation of excessive force is brought forth, other police officers investigate their peers. Only a small number of allegations are recommended for disciplinary action, perhaps in part because peers are investigating them. Thus, this policy change suggests more shared power between civilians and police.

Other voices have called for a solution that would demilitarize the police departments. This suggestion came after police killed protesters in Ferguson using military-level force. Thus, this policy would not allow the use of armored vehicles, drones, or SWAT teams on American citizens unless there is some type of special emergency circumstance that merits it. As part of this, there is also a push to abolish the no-knock raids which allow police to enter someone's home without knocking.

Activists have also called for policies that would limit the use of excessive force by police officers. This means that departments would need to create standards for when force should and should not be used, relying on force only if there is an immediate threat to the life of the officer or someone else in the vicinity. This would push the use of force to the last resort and would have officers rely on more weapons that are not as likely to kills as guns (such as pepper spray, tasers, etc.) as well as de-escalation techniques.

Halting for-profit police work has also been recommended as another way to reform police departments. Currently, many police departments require officers to meet a certain number of quotas for arrests or ticketing. These quotas must typically be met each month by every officer.

Revamping training has also been suggested as another option that should be considered. The pieces of training would increase the number of hours that police officers need to learn about de-escalation techniques. Likewise, it would require officers to purposefully think about racial bias throughout the entire process, from hiring officers to conducting evaluations and reviews, and especially in situations where force may be used.

It is important to note that while many police departments have made efforts to address the excessive use of force, many fail to implement the majority of these recommendations. One or more of these recommendations used in combination could help to significantly alleviate the excessive use of police force against Blacks. It is imperative that police departments carefully consider this problem and address it at all levels including during the hiring process, when training new officers, and when evaluating disciplinary actions after a complaint. This will help ensure safer and more equitable treatment for all American citizens.

65

Chapter 15: Killing Unarmed Black People

George Floyd

The killing of unarmed Black people is sadly not new. The murder of George Floyd reignited a heated debate about the excessive force that police officers dole out to minorities. George Floyd was a 46-year-old male who was being stopped for using one counterfeit bill at a convenience store. This occurred in Minneapolis, Minnesota where Floyd was living at the time of his death. Police were called to the scene and once police officer, Lane, handcuffed him. After Floyd was informed he was under arrest, he was led across the street. He collapsed next to the police car and informed the officers on the scene that he suffers from claustrophobia. He told police officers he was having trouble breathing. Next, Chauvin, another police officer on the scene put his knee on Floyd's neck and kept it there for eight minutes, pinning his head to the ground and reducing airflow. Witnesses attempted to film the incident, but they were instructed to stop filming. Floyd repeatedly said he was unable to breathe. Eventually, an ambulance was called. While waiting for the ambulance, witnesses expressed concern and asked officers to check his pulse. One officer checked and was unable to find a pulse, yet no medical assistance was provided by any of the officers on the scene. Before dying, Floyd had asked for his mama, said he could not breathe, and asked officers not to kill him. Despite all this, George Floyd still died.

When the cause of death for Floyd was reported as a cardiopulmonary arrest during retainment by police, the officers on the scene faced criminal charges. Chauvin is being charged with second-degree murder and manslaughter while the three other officers who were there are being charged with aiding and abetting the murder of Floyd for failing to intervene.

The murder of George Floyd incited energized protests all over the country and even throughout the world. Protesters have called for an end to the use of excessive force and brutality against Blacks. Many of these protests were peaceful at first but later changed when looting began. As such, police responded by using rubber bullets, tear gas, and smoke bombs in multiple cities. Washington, D.C., Denver, Chicago, Los Angeles, and other major cities implemented curfews to keep the protests under control and to prevent looting.

Eric Garner

Much like George Floyd, Eric Garner also died when he was unable to breathe during his arrest due to excessive force in New York. Eric Garner was killed in the summer of 2014. Initially, Garner was arrested because he was allegedly selling single cigarettes without the proper permission to do so. Garner denied these claims and pulled his arms away from the police as they attempted to arrest him. An officer named Pantaleo then put Garner into something known as a chokehold to get him to comply. Garner said eleven times words that would later reverberate across the globe and become a protest slogan – "I can't breathe." Garner lost consciousness yet the chokehold continued. He later died after being transported by ambulance to a local hospital.

Like George Floyd, Garner also had underlying health conditions, including asthma, obesity, and heart problems which combined with the use of a chokehold led to his death. The officer who put Garner into a chokehold, Pantaleo, was not indicted for the murder of Eric Garner, which led to nationwide protests. A settlement of close to six million dollars was reached with Garner's family and the police department was reached after the family filed a civil suit. Pantaleo was fired from his position in the police department five years after the death of Garner.

Freddie Gray

Freddie Gray was a 25-year-old Black man who was killed during a police transport. In this case, the officers failed to provide adequate safety protocols. Gray was arrested for carrying a knife while he was out in Baltimore City. Witness accounts related that police officers were bending Gray to fit him into the police van for transport. During the next 30 minutes, the events that unfolded are unclear. At one point, Gray was put into leg shackles. At some point during this ride, Gray become unresponsive and at the police station, paramedics attempted to revive Gray for more than twenty minutes before he was taken to the emergency room of a local hospital. When he arrived at the hospital he was in a coma.

Gray had fatal neck injuries. It was later determined that Gray had a cardiopulmonary arrest after which he never again becomes conscious. During the next several days, he was operated upon by doctors who attempted to resuscitate him to no avail. Gray had suffered major damage to his spine, voice box, and had several fractured vertebrae all from injuries sustained during transport. The medical examiner later ruled his death a homicide as it resulted from injuries that could have been prevented had proper restraints been used during transport.

In total, six officers were indicted. The charges varied from manslaughter to second-degree murder. All six officers were tried separately and the first officer to go to trial had his case end in a mistrial. The next three officers were acquitted of any wrongdoing. The cases of the remaining officers were dropped. Gray's family eventually settled with Baltimore City for over six million dollars.

The death of Freddie Gray led to major protests in Baltimore and all over the country. Soon after the family held a funeral for Gray, looting, arson, and massive protests swept the streets of Baltimore which resulted in the deployment of the national guard, the implementation of a curfew, and other protective measures. In addition to protests, Freddie Gray has been remembering in pop culture through a documentary called *Baltimore Rising* about his death and in the following songs: *Baltimore, Beautiful Strangers, and Blues for Freddie Gray*.

Breonna Taylor

Breonna Taylor never knew what was coming. She was asleep in her bed in Louisville, Kentucky when police barged into her home in March of 2020. They had been authorized to enter her home using a no-knock warrant, meaning that Breonna had no idea that anyone would be entering her home. Much like anyone in that situation, Breonna's boyfriend sought to defend them from what he thought were intruders coming into her home. He shot his gun and police officers returned fire and ended up shooting Breonna eight times. The warrant, which was originally issued for her boyfriend, included her home, to allow police to search for drugs but none were found in the home.

In addition to using a no-knock warrant, police also made other questionable decisions. For example, the incident report they filed was missing critical information such as the injuries that Breonna sustained. An investigation into the three officers is underway and they are currently on administrative leave while the investigation takes place. In the meantime, Breonna's family has filed a wrongful death lawsuit.

Protests occurred in Louisville which drew hundreds of marchers. These protests later led to looting and eventually with the shooting of multiple protestors. To prevent what happened to Breonna from happing to anyone else, the *Justice in Policing Act of 2020* has been introduced and if passed, it would require that officers announce themselves before entering someone's home. Likewise, Louisville abolished the use of no-knock warrants after Breonna's death. Breonna Taylor will be remembered as a wonderful friend, daughter, and sister as well as for her work as a hospital medical technician. Her untimely death continues to draw attention to the problem of the use of excessive force and for holding police officers accountable for their actions.

Natasha McKenna

Joining the long line of unarmed Blacks who died while in police custody, Natasha McKenna was killed in February 2015. Natasha's case was somewhat different than the previous cases discussed, in that Natasha had a documented history of mental health issues for which she was being treated. Namely, since her teenage years, Natasha dealt with depression, schizophrenia, and bipolar disorder.

At the time of her death, Natasha was just 37 years old. Her untimely death came after she called the police on January 25 of 2015. Her intent in calling the police was to make a report of an assault. A local police officer in Fairfax County, Virginia responded and accompanied her to the hospital for an examination. She also encountered other individuals at the hospital, such as victim specialists, detectives, and doctors. She declined to continue to pursue an investigation and claimed that she did not want the police involved. While police were assisting her, they realized that there was an outstanding felony warrant for her related to assaulting a police officer, stemming from an encounter that occurred about a week and a half earlier.

Early on January 26th, 2015, McKenna was taken to the Fairfax Detention Center for processing and a call was placed to explore transferring her to the Alexandria jurisdiction. This facility was able to provide better medical services for McKenna's mental health needs. However, there was a lengthy delay in the transfer.

On February 3, 2015, McKenna was slated to be transferred to Alexandria. Due to a history of aggression, special measures were taken to protect the police response team charged with transporting her. She allegedly became aggressive which resulted in six officers going to her cell. Measures used included handcuffs and shackling her legs. During this time, one officer used a taser on McKenna and the six officers also used special measures to prevent her from spitting on officers.

McKenna continued to resist efforts to transport her to the new facility, in what was later determined to be a schizophrenic episode. In total, a taser was used on her four times to get her to comply with being put into a restraint chair with wheels. As a result of the tasering, McKenna experienced cardiac arrest and stopped breathing. She was taken to Inova Fairfax Hospital where efforts were made to resuscitate her. However, doctors noted that she was brain dead and her family made the decision to remove her from life support on February 8th, 2015.

Disability advocates argued that McKenna's case could have been handled much better, especially given her mental health history. Having a history of mental health needs was not the unique aspect of this case; there was also a video recording of the events that led up to McKenna's death. They clearly show that excessive force and restraints were used in McKenna's case and documented how many volts of electricity McKenna's body took before she was no longer able to tolerate it.

A comprehensive investigation was conducted related to the actions of officers, the amount of force they used, and the precautions they took. However, no charges were filed as McKenna's death was classified as excited delirium associated with the use of a taser as opposed to directly resulting from the taser. The lack of charges being filed resulted in protests and more calls for just treatment of Blacks with mental illness in the prison system. Natasha left behind a young daughter at the time of her death.

Tanisha Anderson

Like McKenna, Tanisha Anderson was in her late 30s and lived with mental illness. Anderson, who was diagnosed with bipolar disorder in her 20s, tragically also died at the hands of the police who used excessive force when attempting to arrest her. Tanisha Anderson was experiencing a bad episode of mental health symptoms on November 13th, 2015. Her family called the police and two officers responded and treated her with compassion. Things seemed to improve. However, after they left, Tanisha began experiencing additional symptoms. Her family again called 911 and two different police officers were sent to her Cleveland home. The lack of compassion and excessive force used by the last two officers who were sent to her home caused Tanisha's untimely death and traumatized her family who watched as she died before ever reaching the hospital.

The officers attempted to take Tanisha to their police car. It is also important to note that the family was expecting an ambulance to transport Tanisha to a hospital to get treatment for her exacerbating mental health symptoms, but a police car arrived instead. Tanisha was handcuffed. The officers were having trouble getting her into their squad car, so at one point they used a special move to get her to comply. This involved one of the police officers putting his weight on her by kneeling on her back using what is known as a prone position. Tanisha, the once lively mother, and lovely daughter and sister lost consciousness at this point and would never recover. Before taking her last breath, she yelled for her brother and mother to help her.

In the coming days, Tanisha's death was determined to be a homicide associated with the physical restraint used by police officers. Tanisha had medical conditions, including bipolar disorder and heart problems, which also contributed to her death in conjunction with the type of restraint that officers used on her. However, this initial cause of death was later investigated and a second evaluation into Tanisha's cause of death was conducted. The second evaluation determined that her death was related to a cardiac event.

Tanisha's death also highlighted the inappropriate treatment of people with mental illness. A subsequent report showed that these particular officers, as well as most other officers on the Cleveland Police Force, failed to use adequate de-escalation techniques before resorting to the use of excessive force against individuals who have special medical and mental health needs.

The arresting officers were ultimately cleared by a grand jury and did not face charges for her death. One officer received a written warning and was suspended from his job for just ten days. Both officers received disciplinary action for failing to call for an ambulance sooner. Several years after her tragic death, Anderson's family settled with the city for a $2.25 million-dollar settlement with the circumstances surrounding her death.

Antwon Rose Jr.

Antwon Rose was a smart young man who was on the Honor Roll. He was out riding in a car with friends when police pulled the car over. Antwon and one other passenger ran from the car. Instead of running after him, the police officer shot at Antwon three times, hitting him with each shot. Rose's case was unique in that another motorist provided a recording of the stop. She asked on the recording why they were shooting at him just for running. It is a question that remains unanswered.

The officer who shot Rose had not been properly trained. He had faced disciplinary action at his previous precinct. The medical examiner determined that Rose died from a gunshot wound and classified his cause of death as murder, thus forcing the officer responsible to stand trial. However, the officer was found not guilty at the trial.

The acquittal of the officer who shot Rose results in upheaval and protests in Pittsburg. These protests continued for days after the death and again after the acquittal of the officer responsible for the shooting. After the acquittal, Rose's family filed a civil lawsuit for wrongful death against the city that employed this police officer. Rose's family was indeed successful in their pursuit of the settlement. It is reported that there was a $2 million settlement reached.

Part of the settlement cited that the officer did not have adequate reason to detain Rose. Additionally, it claimed that excessive force was used when the officer shot the 17-year-old three times for no reason. It would have been possible to detain him without the use of deadly force. The suit also claimed that racial bias on behalf of the officer played a role in the events that led to Rose's death. The lawsuit also alleged that the officer did not receive proper training.

His mother remembers her son by holding an annual birthday celebration to honor his life. Her hope is that fosters community cohesion through free food and donations to the community. However, the loss of this young life still reverberates throughout the state. Unfortunately, not much has changed since the death of Antwon Rose regarding holding police accountable for their use of excessive force against unarmed Black people. Likewise, there is still a way to go in terms of providing adequate training to new officers on de-escalation techniques.

"Say Their Names" Campaign

Several campaigns have stemmed from the unjustified killing of unarmed Black people. One of those is the #SayHerName campaign that was started in 2014. This campaign is jointly sponsored by the Center for Intersectionality and Social Policy Studies as well as the African American Policy Forum. This campaign ensures that Black women and girls who were killed by police are not forgotten. In some cases, the families of the victims also receive support from these organizations. Using this hashtag, victims are remembered online. Additionally, there have been various in-person vigils throughout the country where names are said out loud to remember the victims, including annual events on Mother's Day.

"Say Their Names" Campaign is a spinoff of the #SayHerName Campaign and is more inclusive of including Black men and women who were tragically killed due to racism, the use of excessive force, and/or due to other social injustices. Various fundraisers have been started under this heading, selling shirts, quilts, and other apparel, with the names of those who were lost too soon. Proceeds typically go to support causes fighting to end police brutality or racism, such as Black Lives Matter.

Chapter 16: Looting Laws

Is looting a crime?

Sometimes people are confused about whether looting is a crime. Part of the confusion comes into play because they are widely different state and local laws regarding looting, not to mention laws that vary significantly by country. In the United States, looting is indeed a crime. In fact, during times of emergency, police officers have been given the authority to shoot at looters. For example, after Hurricane Katrina hit New Orleans, looting was becoming rampant. There was so much chaos amid a city that had been truly devastated by flooding. So many people lost everything. To restore order, police in New Orleans were given the okay to shoot looters. One man named Henry Glover was indeed shot while he was looting goods. Most of the time, looting after natural disasters tends to be treated with more leniency than looting during other times.

In addition to the confusing variation among state and local laws, another factor that makes it challenging to understand looting laws is that looting is not ever what the person is charged with. Rather, looting is more of an umbrella term that encapsulates many other charges. For example, a looter could be charged with breaking, stealing, burglary, vandalism, or a wide variety of other charges. The severity of the charges can range from misdemeanors to felony charges. There tend to be more penalties when officers are attempting to restore order amid chaos, such as when protests become unruly or when people are becoming hurt or injured during demonstrations.

In a moral consideration of looting, it is always a crime. The mere definition of looting implies that someone is taking or destroying something that does not belong to him or her. So regardless of whether the act of looting involved breaking a storefront glass window, stealing groceries or goods, vandalizing a building with graffiti, or some combination of these acts, there is a loss and/or devaluation of someone else's belonging. Additionally, the person committing the act did not have the other person's authorization to incur the damage or destruction. Therefore, in addition to facing a variety of criminal charges stemming from the looting incident, there is also the moral contention that looting is wrong.

Often looters engage in acts that are meant to bring more attention to their cause. If that is the case, consider that police are likely to respond with significant consequences that could put your life or their lives in danger. Additionally, often local citizens are likely to respond with fear. Thus, will looting often does make headlines it does little to further the cause the looter is trying to bring to the forefront and can result in heavy fines or jail time for those found guilty of looting.

Examples of Varying State Looting Laws

As mentioned previously, looting laws can vary dramatically across state lines. In this section, we explore more in-depth what those differing laws look like. To begin exploring, we head to California to better understand the penalties for looting. California has separate looting laws for instances that occur under a "state of emergency" designation, such as wildfires, riot, or flood. In those cases, California imposes a second-degree burglary charge to the looter at minimum, but other charges may be applicable. In California, the looting that is designated as a misdemeanor typically results in about a year sentence in county jail. However, there are much longer penalties for felony sentences, which generally range from 16 months to several years. These are known as wobbler offenses.

In California, several factors can help you lower the amount of time or money you owe during the sentencing phase. For example, if the police did not adhere to "search and seizure" laws or if you lacked intent to commit the looting, then you are eligible to receive a lower sentence. Petty theft charges in the state result in monetary fines of no more than $1,000 and at least three months in county jail. Felony charges can result in up to $10,000 in monetary fines.

California also has special laws that require officers to use the least amount of force possible when arresting looters, but this is not the case in all states. In Texas, looting laws became stricter in 2017 after Hurricane Harvey hit and caused mass destruction. Looters faced additional years of imprisonment if they were found guilty of looting in Texas during times of crisis. Texas allows individuals to carry guns (either concealed or openly) for the week following any natural disaster.

In Texas, much of the sentencing is determined by the amount that the property was stolen is worth. For example, if a looter takes something valued at less than $100, the looter would receive a $500 fine which is a class C misdemeanor. However, if the stolen property is worth $30,000 or more, the looter could face a maximum of a $10,000 fine and up to ten years in jail. However, burglary charges could also be added which carries a term of life in prison.

Looting during the State of Emergency

Looting during states of emergency can result in more severe punishment when it comes to sentencing. That is because states and police forces are attempting to keep everyone safe and prevent looting. Likewise, people's homes and businesses are more at risk when there are power outages, severe damage, and other environmental factors. When it is not safe for people to be in the area, evacuation orders may go into effect. This makes it impossible for homeowners and business owners to check on their property, which makes an opportune time for looting.

As mentioned previously, in Louisiana after Hurricane Katrina police officers had more flexibility in shooting looters, which would not normally be allowed. Likewise, after Hurricane Harvey, individual citizens were allowed to carry concealed guns to protect themselves and their property. Other states also impose similar penalties during states of emergency and call in additional support, such as The National Guard, to help protect citizens.

Possible Punishments for Looting

When determining punishments for looting, many factors are taken into account. The first is whether there was intent to commit a crime. A second important factor to consider in the context of the crime; such as whether it was looting based on a need for survival or needless looting to cause destruction. Likewise, the context of the looting is important and considers whether the looting occurred during a major natural disaster or state of emergency, and if it did, the consequences will likely be harsher than if the looting occurred during times of peace.

In Washington, D.C., during the George Floyd protests, there have been some arrests of people due to looting. However, thus far, there have been no charges stemming from these incidents. In other places, it is also possible that looters are let go without being charged. However, in the vast majority of looting cases, looters will face misdemeanor charges when the value of the items stolen is minimal. However, fines of up to $10,000, and jail time of up to 25 years can be imposed for felony looting.

When thinking about punishments for looting, as a reminder, it is important to think about associated charges as well and how that might impact the sentencing. For example, burglary charges can carry up to life in jail and even heavier fines. Each state will have its own rules and regulations around sentencing. Likewise, each state has its factors that mitigate or increase the sentence, such as whether anyone was injured, the value of the property, and whether there was intent to commit the crime.

What to do if you are accused of Looting

Perhaps you attended what you thought would be a peaceful protest for a cause dear to your heart when those you were with began looting. You are arrest along with others. What should you do?

Regardless of whether or not you intended to loot, the first thing you should do is ask for a lawyer. As you have read in this book so far, looting charges are nothing to laugh at and can have serious, life-altering consequences. Thus, you should take the allegations very seriously. During times of crisis, police departments may be stretched thin and you could end up getting caught in a lose-lose situation without legal counsel.

After contacting a lawyer, go over the details of your case. Your lawyer will help you understand what you are being charged with. Ask your lawyer whether any mitigating or exceptional factors can help your case. For example, in the vignette above the person did not know their peers were going to loot and therefore did not go into the situation to loot, which is a mitigating factor in some states. Ask about the state and local laws that pertain to your case and develop a plan with your lawyer about how to proceed.

Chapter 17: How to Defend Your Home or Business from Looting

Steps to take to defend your home from looting

During times of unrest, many homeowners and business owners may become fearful of being looted. This can occur when people see news stories on television or read articles in the newspaper about nearby looting. It can also occur when masses of people are protesting unjust treatment, such as racism, police brutality, abortion rights, or other issues that people want to be taken seriously. With so many people in one city or space, it can become challenging for police to monitor property and to adequately intervene. For example, during the Atlanta protests when protesters were demonstrating over the death of Rayshard Brooks, someone started a fire at the Wendy's where Brooks had been shot. Protestors blocked a major interstate, which prevented police and emergency responders, including firefighters from accessing the fire. Thus, the police decided to let the fire continue, and Wendy's burned down. That was in part because firefighters would have needed police back-up to get through the protesters on the interstate, which could have caused additional problems.

So, if you are a homeowner or business owner, how can you protect yourself? It helps if you spend some time thinking through safety precautions and protocols that you can take before a riot or looting occurs. Here are some tried and true methods of keeping your home and business safe from looters:

Use Heavy-Duty Locks

When it comes to home safety, you want the best for you and your family. Instead of opting for low-cost locks that do little to prevent break-ins, invest in heavy-duty locks. Some higher-tech locks have night lockdown options and secure themselves into the floor or wall to prevent the door from being opened. Heavy-duty locks typically have additional features that make it hard for someone to break in or pick a lock. Choose stainless steel locks. Make sure that you monitor who is getting a key to the lock and do not leave extra keys hidden around your home. This will help minimize the likelihood of looters finding a key or breaking in if you have to temporarily abandon your home due to a state of emergency. When choosing heavy-duty locks, also think about how to best secure your home in case of power outages, during which home security systems will be down.

Instead of Glass, Use Plexiglass

One of the most vulnerable spots for any home is windows. By simply breaking the glass, looters or burglars can gain easy entry into your home. How can you prevent this? One simple option is to replace all of your glass windows with plexiglass. Plexiglass is much more durable than glass. It is up to 17 times more durable than glass. If you and your family are home when looters try to break in, you will have some warning to prepare yourselves, call for help, or escape. Plexiglass may eventually crack, but it will take longer to break than glass.

If you want extra security for your home, in addition to the plexiglass or glass windows, add some steel bars. These are very popular options in Europe and other countries outside the United States for securing the home. If you have glass or plexiglass, even if someone can break through it, the addition of steel bars will prevent the looter from going into your home. Thus, they would only be able to take what they can reach via arm's length from between the bars.

Get a Guard Dog

Throughout history, people have used guard dogs as a way to alert them when something is amiss. The barking of a dog has been known to scare off intruders who are hoping to enter your home quietly. If you do opt for a guard dog, know that not all breeds are equally good when it comes to protecting you, your family, and your home. Certain breeds stand out as being among the best in terms of guard dogs. The best guard dogs are Chesapeake Bay Retrievers, Rottweilers, Doberman Pinschers, and Akita. You have likely seen one or more of these breeds depicted as guard dogs in movies or television shows.

If you opt for a guard dog, you will want to make sure to socialize your dog so it is friendly towards you, your family, and your guests. You will need to teach your dog to defend you from strangers, but you will also want a command that alerts your dog to stop barking and calm down in case the person is someone you know. Consider obedience classes to help you in this endeavor. To protect against looters, you can also put "Beware of Dog" signs up in your yard and teach your dog to bark when he or she sees someone in your yard.

Keep Surrounding Area Well Lit

This tip should come as no surprise to homeowners. You have likely seen this tip from well-meaning neighborhood watch groups, condo associations, or other security alerts. When it comes to looting, theft, and breaking, thieves look for dark areas. They do not want to be seen and they do not want to be recorded. It is much easier to get away with looting when it is done in the dark, clandestinely.

To avoid this, keep the area around your home well lit. This means having lighting on the exterior of your home. Also, think through what would happen during periods of extended power outages. Consider also investing in some LED outdoor lighting or solar-powered lights. These could help light your garden, mailbox, pathway, or drive around your home.

When making a plan for outdoor lighting, ensure that there is adequate light around any entry point to your home. This includes your front door, back entrance, and garage. Make sure that any side entrances are also covered. One fun option to keep windows, decks, or patios brightly illuminated is to use decorative string lights. You can also consider putting some lights on a timer so that it is more unpredictable when the lights will be on and off.

Other Steps

When it comes to protecting everything, you have worked so hard for, you want to know that you are taking all possible steps. Aside from using heavy-duty locks, getting a guard dog, and keeping the surrounding area well lit, what else can you do? The first is to make sure you and your family will be safe. Set up one or two areas in the home where you will have access to a phone to call for help, water, and other emergency supplies. After that, you will want something to defend your home with. Consider purchasing pepper spray or mace to deter looters. In some states, it is also legal to use a gun to defend yourself.

One important thing to note is that many states do not allow the use of booby traps and will often hold the homeowner accountable if an intruder is injured through the use of a booby trap. Instead, consider setting up a camera or security alert that will allow you to capture the intruder in action. Another popular option is to join together with neighbors to create a neighborhood watch or to have a security patrol in your neighborhood.

Steps to take to defend your business from looting

If looting breaks out in your area of business what will you do? Some things to keep in mind when thinking through this is how you can best prepare if you are unable to access the area near your business (in case of rioting, police blockades, etc.) or what to do if you are stuck at your business when looting starts. Both of these present different and unique challenges to think through. In one case, you want to prevent intruders from getting inside, while in the second case you also want to make sure those inside remain safe.

Luckily, there are many proactive steps that you can take to keep your business safe, whether or not you are there. While it does take some planning and forethought to set up these measures, they can pay off big time if looters are unable to target your business due to the security measures. Here are some tips on how to protect your business from being looted:

Use Security Cameras

While this may seem simple, you would be surprised by how many places of business do not use security cameras. If you do not already have one, now is the time to invest! Simply having security cameras alone does not mean you are protected. There are several things you need to think through.

First, you should think through the placement of the security videos. Will the intruder be able to hide from the camera? If so, the camera will not help you identify those responsible for the looting or give a description to police officers about who they are looking for. You want to make sure that the security camera or cameras are set up to get a good angle of the intruders.

Secondly, you will want to think about how many security cameras you need. This depends in large part on the size of your business and the layout of the building. At a minimum, you will likely want one security camera outside your place of business and one inside your business. The outside camera can help capture graffiti artists or vandals that exclusively indoor security cameras would miss. You will want to try to position the outdoor security cameras so that there is a good view of the entry points to your business. Indoor security camera locations should be thought through strategically as well. What if someone loots your building but is not captured on one security camera. Would having cameras at different locations, at different heights, and capturing different angles help? It is unlikely that someone would be able to bypass multiple cameras without being seen, but there is a good chance that he or she could get past one camera.

When thinking about security cameras, it is also important to think about how the footage is stored. If someone breaks in and disables the security camera, will you still have the footage or is the footage only stored on-site? If the on-site storage is not secured, the looters could just take off with the footage and you would have no recourse. Thus, it is best to look into cameras that offer the option of off-site recordings or off-site back-ups so that if a looter takes the camera, you will still be able to see what is happening or has occurred.

Aside from the points mentioned above, security cameras often deter crime. If a potential looter sees a camera, he or she will be more reluctant to enter and may choose a business that does not have those security measures in place. You can also add a signature to your business indicating that the site is being monitored by security cameras.

Call the Police when intruders are present

This may seem like common sense, but people often forget this step. Sometimes when intruders enter, people may freeze. If possible, try to make it to a phone to call the police as soon as possible. Calmly tell them your business address, your name, and where you are located in your building or office space. If you are monitoring the site from offsite and notice activity on your security camera, you will also want to alert police to the presence of intruders.

If it is possible, police will generally respond quickly to requests for assistance. If there is rioting or other unrest that makes it difficult for them to get to you, follow their advice. If you are in the building, this will likely include finding a safe space and staying on the phone with the police. If you are off-site, the police may ask you to continue monitoring and safe any footage of the intruders for a later investigation.

Hire Extra Security Personnel

When it comes to safety, you can never be too careful. While this step may not be necessary for all businesses, it can be incredibly helpful as a preventative measure. If there is an increase in looting or rioting around your area of business, you can consider supplementing your security team with extra temporary patrol officers. If you do not already have a security team, you can opt to hire one for the short term. Businesses such as banks, jewelry stores, and other high-end businesses tend to have some sort of security guards to protect their assets. If potential looters see a security guard, they are likely to think twice about looting at that site.

Texas Deadly Force

Sometimes business owners wonder if they are allowed to use deadly force to protect their property. This question depends on which state you live in. Throughout the majority of the United States, using deadly force against looters is illegal, and should you choose to ignore it, you could be facing murder charges. This may seem illogical to you. However, most states agree that deadly force should not be used to protect property and should be reserved only if one's life is being threatened.

However, there is one exception to this rule. For example, Texas does indeed allow the use of deadly force to protect home or business interests under certain circumstances. It order to use this in Texas, someone must have reason to believe that it is imminently necessary to use deadly force to prevent theft, burglary, robbery, arson, or similar event. Likewise, before using that level of force, the person must believe that the property could not be otherwise protected or recovered if taken. It is imperative to understand when deadly force can be used in Texas, before using it, as it is not allowable under certain circumstances. In all other states, you should refrain from deadly force.

Pepper Spray

This is one of the least costly and most transportable resources for protecting your business. Purchasing pepper spray online or at any outdoor store is fairly inexpensive. There are pepper spray containers that can easily clip onto your key chain, belt, or wallet.

You can leave containers of pepper spray at your store, in certain designated locations, so that if you or your employees find themselves at the business with a looter there is one option for self-protection that relies on minimal force. Make sure the containers are easily accessible to employees and that you know how to use the pepper spray.

Spraying the pepper spray in when an intruder enters will make it challenging for the intruder to see or smell. It will also irritate the throat. When you spray it, aim it towards their face and try to cover your face. If it has distracted the looter, you can either flee or call for help.

Add steel bars to windows

Another relatively simple step to beef up security around the premises of your business is to add steel bars. This should be done around any windows or doorways. Adding steel bars to the windows will make it difficult for someone to enter through the windows, which is one of the most common ways looters enter into businesses. Even if they break the glass, their entire body will not fit through the steel bars. Adding a steel door, in addition to your main door, will have the same effect as making it impossible for a looter to fit their body through the opening.

Of particular importance when considering steel bars are the large storefront glass windows, which are commonly broken during looting. If possible, try to add a drop-down gate that goes into the front of the glass and prevents people from entering.

Other Steps

The steps above are just a few possible steps that you can take to prevent looters from entering your business. Some of the steps mentioned in the home protection area, also apply to businesses. For example, ensuring good lighting and getting a guard dog can both aid in looting prevention efforts.

There are additional steps you can take as well. First, make sure not to leave money in the cash register at your store. You can even put a sign up that no cash is on the premises. Keep doors locked and limit who has access to spare keys. You want to minimize the opportunity for people who should not be in your business to enter. Use ink tags or sensors on expensive merchandise so that you hear or see when looters are trying to make off with your merchandise. As mentioned in a previous section, you can use plexiglass instead of glass to prevent break-ins. You can also form a coalition with neighboring businesses and take turns checking on businesses in the area.

You may not need to employ all of the steps described here to protect your business. However, you must think through a safety plan for your business and modify that as needed, depending on current events. For example, many people had little time to prepare for stay at home orders that accompanied the coronavirus. However, many businesses had plans in place to ensure that they continued to operate and deter intruders and looters.

Chapter 18: Destroying their Neighborhood as a Form of Protest

One of the most surprising aspects of protesting is when protestors act in ways that destroy their neighborhood or resources. Intuitively, people would expect protestors to target other neighborhoods while protecting their own at all costs. However, this has not always happened. Next, we explore why people would destroy their neighborhood and whether it is done intentionally or unintentionally.

Why would anyone destroy their neighborhood?

When you think of protestors vandalizing areas, you never imagine that they vandalize their neighborhood. But in fact, that has been occurring, even more so after the Gorge Floyd protests. What causes this? Some people have suggested the social experiments conducted by psychologists have suggested that when neighborhoods look run down, people will not respect them. In the majority of cases, people who are protesting are doing so because of disparities in terms of neighborhoods, schools, power, and other social disparities.

Another theory is that people destroy their neighborhoods to gain attention for the cause. Indeed, when stores are lit on fire, when people are forced out of their homes, and when small businesses are forced to close due to excessive damages, headlines will be made. The fact is that these protests are often incited by true anger over injustices and systematic oppression, rather than an intention to destroy.

Do people destroy their neighborhood intentionally or unintentionally when protesting?

Most people do not set out to destroy their neighborhoods. As discussed above, what happens in the majority of cases is that individuals plan to protest some injustice that they have experienced. In many cases, these are historic injustices that have occurred on many occasions, throughout time. Their experience with attempting to address their concerns through formal means has been ignored or invalidated. Thus, they turn to protest.

Most protests are peaceful. When people resort to destroying their neighborhood, it is often not planned. When people become very angry about the causes they are passionate about, it can result in impulsive behavior. Likewise, it can be a response to the police or other officials' treatment of the protestors. There are many reasons why people might destroy their neighborhood, but it is often not intentional.

Chapter 19: Examples of Protests Related to Looting Around the World

For centuries, people have been protesting all over the world. This universal reaction to injustice has helped affect change all over the country and even the world. The most recent example of this can be seen in the protests related to the death of George Floyd.

George Floyd Protests and Looting

As previously discussed, George Floyd was a Black man living in Minneapolis. For over eight minutes, he implored a White police officer to remove his knee from his neck. He repeatedly told the officer that he was unable to breathe. However, the officer did not remove his knee from Floyd's neck until after Floyd lost consciousness. Bystanders attempted to intervene and help Floyd, but they were threatened and told to stop recording the incident as well. This all occurred because Floyd allegedly used a counterfeit $20 at a local store.

Vocal protests have been occurring all over the United States in reaction to Floyd's death. Indeed, Floyd joins a long line of Black victims who met their untimely death at the hands of police officers, who use excessive force to restrain suspects. As part of the protests, people are taking to the streets to demand equal treatment for Black people as well as to stop the use of excessive force by police officers. One unique aspect of the events and protests that have stemmed from the Floyd protests is that for the first time, the protesters come from all different walks of life and are more diverse than ever before. What started as protesting for Black Lives Matter, has shifted into a movement that encapsulates anyone who feels that discrimination is incurring in America.

In the United States, the Floyd protests led to rioting and looting, although most started peacefully. Washington, D.C., and Los Angeles, CA were just two of the many cities that had to impose curfews to minimize the damage. In Washington, D.C. people who did not adhere to curfews were arrested. Rubber bullets and tear gas spread throughout major U.S. cities as police tried to keep the protests under control.

While protesters were taking to the streets to advocate for Floyd, the death of Rayshard Brooks occurred which caused, even more, protesting, riots and looting. In Atlanta, GA, where Brooks was killed at the hands of police who also allegedly used excessive force, there was a contentious standoff with police and protesters. At one point, protestors blocked seven lanes of a major highway. While this was occurring, someone set fire to the establishment where Brooks had been killed.

The protests for George Floyd have not been limited to the United States. Protests have been occurring in more than one hundred different locations around the world. In Africa, protests have been mounted by people in Kenya, Ghana, Nigeria, and Liberia at their respective U.S. Embassies. People in Taiwan, South Korea, and China also joined in peaceful protests to advocate for human rights. Many countries in Europe also lent support to the movement, with people from Bulgaria, Austria, France, Greece, Denmark, and other countries protesting. In Belgium and some other countries, luxury shops were looted as part of the protest.

Hurricane Katrina Looting

Hurricane Katrina causes devastation on of unimaginable proportions with no warning. When the levees broke, people had no time to prepare for the massive flooding that came. Many people lost their homes or businesses that they had worked their entire lives to build. Thus, it is not surprising that many people became desperate and turned to other means to acquire the goods they needed. Likewise, other people who did not need anything simply took advantage of a unique situation to loot items they wanted to profit from the misfortune.

With floodwaters coming to their hips, some looters waded through the streets to obtain their loot. This included grocery items from pharmacies and apparel from clothing stores. Some people attempted to hide what they were doing out of shame or embarrassment, while others looted goods right from under the noses of neighbors and police officers.

Some people justified the looting claiming they needed the items to survive. And in some cases that may have been true. After Katrina hit, rescue workers had a very difficult time moving people to safety. As a result, many people left behind died. Some people chose not to evacuate due to fear of looting which further endangered their lives, while others who did leave ended up having their homes or businesses looted.

Mexico Gas Prices Looting and Protesting

Several years ago, protests broke out in Mexico in response to a huge spike in gasoline prices. The price of gas increased significantly, in some cases as much as 20%. As part of the protesting efforts, coordinated blockades of roads were conducted. Additionally, there was plenty of looting and vandalism. People stole everything from toys to groceries, to gasoline when the looting occurred. There were several hundreds of people who were arrested in response to these protests. Unfortunately, there were also some fatalities among protesters.

Greece and Archeological looting

Throughout history, some civilizations have experienced looting more than others. Greece is one of those civilizations. Due to their tremendous archeological history, looting has long been part of Greek history. Given the recent economic decline in Greece, more people are turning towards looting Greek antiquities than ever before. More and more people are looking for ancient coins or very old artifacts using metal detectors. For a country that is incredibly wealthy in terms of artifacts, police struggle to keep up with the looting.

Martin Luther King and Protests

Martin Luther King was a leader of the civil rights movement that occurred in the mid-1950s through the late 1960s. He is best known for his "I Have a Dream" speech and how he envisioned a future America for his children where people of every race were treated equally. Although he engaged in protests and encouraged others to do so as well, he put forth a nonviolent protest to draw attention to his cause. His stance on nonviolence was influenced from the viewpoints of the notable Mahatma Gandhi. His inspirational views attracted thousands of followers to promote the idea that Blacks and Whites should have equal rights. He even won the Nobel Peace Prize for effective racial change through the use of nonviolence.

Martin Luther King Jr. was killed in 1968. He was assassinated by James Ray at his hotel room in Tennessee, where he was slated to give a speech. Following the assassination of Martin Luther King, Jr., Robert F. Kennedy who was running for the office of the president, implored people to protest peacefully and in the nonviolent fashion that King sought to use. King and his work are eternally memorialized through the establishment of Martin Luther King Jr. Day, which occurs every year on the third Monday of January. His legacy of committing to nonviolent action has been pushed to the forefront in early 2020, with the protests relating to Black Lives Matter and the George Floyd protests.

Boston Tea Party

The Boston Tea Party occurred in the state of Massachusetts in 1773. In this case, protesters were opposed to the Tea Act of May 10, 1773, and sought to make their political views known. The act enabled tea from the Chinese empire to be sold throughout America without paying taxes. As a result of this, more than thirty protesters boarded a boat carrying a new shipment of this tea as it entered Boston Harbor and threw large quantities of tea into the harbor below.

In response to this act, the British government denounced the act. This subsequently escalated into the American Revolution. Another result of this protest was that throughout America, tea-drinking fell and more Americans began drinking coffee. This demonstrates how a small, coordinated protest can incite long-lasting change as well as lead to escalation depending upon the response of the government.

London Riots August, 2011

One of the most memorable protests and looting incidents of the last decade occurred in London, from August 6 through 11 in 2011. This was caused as a reaction to the police shooting of Mark Duggan on August 4, 2011. Mark Duggan was a young man of mixed race, which would later become an important aspect of how police treat people who are not White. People in London were very dissatisfied with how the attempted arrest of Mark Duggan was handled. To demonstrate this, they began rioting, setting places and things on fire, looting, and destroying the city. There was massive property damage to vehicles, buildings, and homes. In total, more than 3,000 people were arrested and there were sadly five deaths.

These few days were a period of lawlessness in the city of London. There was chaos. The people were angry about racial inequalities and the use of excessive force by police in London. This also came during a time of economic downturn, so some people simply needed items but who were unable to afford them. Additionally, there had been several cuts to public services due to the economic decline.

One unique aspect of the London riots is that there is very detailed information about who was arrested. London has a comprehensive system of cameras spread out across the city. These cameras would later become essential in prosecuting individuals who participated in destroying property. As a result, the London riots resulted in more detailed information about who participates in riots. Those who participated tended to hail from neighborhoods that were the poorest and tended not to have higher education.

Aside from the great network of cameras, police also relied on social media posts since many citizens who participated in the looting had posted on social media. Media coverage and Google Maps were also used as tools to tape footage of what was happening. Thus, in the end, many of those involved were able to be located and prosecuted for their involvement.

Iraq Baghdad Riots After the U.S. Invasion in 2003

When it comes to riots, there is usually some major event that is the catalyst for the riots. In the Baghdad riots that hit Iraq in 2003, this was also the case. Soldiers who had worked for Saddam Hussein began to worry about not receiving payments to which they were entitled. The payments amount to around the U.S. equivalent of $40. For the soldiers, the anxiety began when they heard whispers that they may not be paid due to a lack of funds, a rumor said to have started by the Baathists who wanted to create a disruption. The result was a large number of riots that year which resulted in the loss of lives and financial damage.

However, that was not the only riot in Baghdad in 2003. Riots also broke out across many Iraqi cities to demonstrate opposition to the Iraq War. One of the most well-coordinated, and also largest, protests occurred on February 15th, 2003. One unique aspect of this protest is that they were held all over the world, not just in Iraq. In fact, in total there were over 600 different cities across the world who took part in this protest.

These protests were a response to the 2002 invasion of Iraq by the United States, under the direction of George W. Bush. This came soon after the United States experienced the devastating events of 9/11 when hijackers from the Middle East boarded commercial planes and flew them into both towers of the World Trade Center in New York City, The Pentagon in Washington, D.C., and one other plane whose exact destination remains a mystery since the plane crashed in a field before it could hit its target. Bush sanctioned the Iraq war in part, due to claims of needing to locate weapons of mass destruction.

Many countries joined forces to denounce this war, which was not well-supported even by U.S. allies. The countries taking part in this protest included European countries, such as Greece, Germany, and France, as well as countries in Asia such as China and Japan. There were even protests across many U.S. cities, such as New York City and San Francisco, as well as in Canada. This protest was supported by anti-war organizations.

These protests had some impact in demonstrating the world-wide, collective opposition to this war. However, they did not have the effect of entirely stopping the U.S. invasion of Iraq. So, while the protests were successful in creating the largest protest even across different continents and countries, future protests against the war would become common as this war ended up lasting until 2011 when President Barak Obama pulled troops out.

Looting Art throughout History

Looting throughout history has been happening for many centuries. It is one area of history that is often not well explored. The exact history of looting varies by country. Some of the earliest known looters were robbers who stole from the great and bountiful tombs of the Pharaohs. These tombs contained mummified remains of those who had died, along with food, clothing, jewelry made from gold and other precious metals, and other items of real value.

One country that has been on the receiving end of a great deal of looting is Germany. After the Germans lost the second World War, their country was looted by many forces including Russian and Allied troops. During this time, troops stole millions worth of books, artwork such as sculptures (e.g., Nicola Pisano), paintings by famous people such as Botticelli, and household jewels and treasures.

However, when the Nazi regime was in power, they were also responsible for looting millions of dollars' worth of valuables from the Jewish people they were sent to concentration camps. This included valuable jewelry such as watches, rings, and necklaces. It also included artwork, household goods, money, gold, and inheritances taken from the homes during Nazi raids. In addition to Jewish people, the Nazi's also raided surrounding countries as their reign grew.

Italy has also been on the receiving end of looted artwork since the time of Napoleon. Authorities in Italy have specially trained police to help monitor the taking and sale of looted antiquities. Italy has had success in finding and petitioning for the return of looted artwork, from famous museums abroad such as The Toledo Museum of Art and the Metropolitan Museum of Art.

Chapter 20: How Do Looters See Their Actions?

Have you ever wondered how looters see their actions? Do they think what they are doing in wrong and unjust? Alternatively, are they able to justify their actions to themselves? One school of thought suggests that looters see the option to loot as a way to reclaim their dignity after decades of abuse received at the hands of authorities and police. These are people who have been consistently and persistently denied opportunities based on the color of their skin, their socioeconomic status, or other differences. They may view looting as justified.

So how do looters view their actions? Some researchers who study race relations posit that the loss of human life is incomparable to any amount of stolen goods. Thus, when examples of police brutality go without remedying the problem and those who commit the acts are set free without enough punishment, people turn this sense of unfairness into looting. Aside from this, there are several other ways that looters can describe their actions.

The first is that when they are around others who are engaging in looting, they get caught up in the moment. Thus, their unique morals and ability to reason are not coming into play. They are not thinking through possible options and alternatives in a rational way. Rather, they get caught up with other people in the mob and join in. If they were not with these people, then they would not engage in the looting. It is because of this reason that some cities have special curfews for juveniles during times of civil unrest.

Another reason why people loot is that they feel that it is the only way they can demonstrate their anger. They feel they have exhausted other coping options and that this is the only one that remains. They want the world to know how angry they are about some kind of treatment or injustice they have experienced.

The third reason for looting is simply because there is an opportunity to do so. This most commonly attracts people who come from very low socioeconomic backgrounds and who needs goods but who are unable to afford them. It can also happen after natural disasters when typical security measures put into place by businesses have been compromised.

A fourth reason that people looters want to loot is that they hope that their actions will affect some sort of change. With the current George Floyd protests, looters sometimes hope that the sheer amount of looting, destruction, and demonstrations will garner attention and support for their fight for racial equity. Also, there is a hope to end the excessive use of force against Black people by police forces. Throughout the last couple of decades, there have been too many examples of young Black men and women dying for no reason while in police custody. Thus, looters see their actions as justified to shift attention to the need for change.

While sometimes looters see their actions as justified, the law does not tend to agree with them. Also, looting can detract from the cause for which the protests are occurring. Many organizations, such as Black Lives Matter, speaking out about not condoning looting as they want peaceful protests. Another important aspect of this is that many times peaceful protesters come during the daytime to fight for their cause, but looting occurs by a few people or smaller groups in the evening. These two groups tend to be comprised of disparate people who are coming to the event for different reasons. No matter how looters see their actions, the damage from looting can destroy and disrupt the livelihood of small business owners and can cost the city huge amounts of money. Additionally, it can potentially cost the looter himself or herself a great deal in terms of financial penalties and jail time if caught.

Chapter 21: Journalists have also contributed to the Looting

Some people have claimed that journalists have contributed to the problem of looting. They claim that when violent behaviors are used to obtain media attention and receive media attention, there is an implicit reinforcement of the desired behavior. When it comes to media and looting, there is a lot to think about in terms of the media's role.

The media has an obligation to the public to show, without prejudice, what is happening in the world. This includes looting. However, when looting is done to further an ideological cause or a political cause, looting to obtain media attention can be exacerbated as looters want more and more media coverage. On the flip side, police can use the media's video coverage as one tool to catch those responsible for looting, so they also have an appreciation of media videotapes. These tapes have been successfully used in later prosecuting looters.

In today's world, the media often covers many events that are designed to get media attention. Looting is no different and it is likely to continue whether or not there are media press there or not. Journalists have been harmed during the 2020 George Floyd protests. They have been arrested, hurt by rubber bullets, and in the case of Linda Tirado, even blinded while covering the protests and looting. Journalists have to strike a balance between providing accurate media coverage and maintaining their safety amid chaos.

Chapter 22: Insurance Claims After Riots

The riots of 2020 have shown several questions to the forefront. One question relates to how we can do more to ensure racial equality. Another question focuses on safety and the success of small businesses amid the COVID-19 pandemic. A third, less clear question, relates to who covers the damage done by protesters after riots. This should be placed into the context that many small businesses and even individual property owners have experienced huge financial losses during March through June 2020, when many places were shut down or forced to run on a limited basis due to the pandemic, which resulted into huge monetary losses.

This also coincided with a large increase in the number of riots and protests that occurred across the country. When riots, looting, and protests result in damage to the business, who covers that? Damage could be as minimal as a broken window or graffiti on the outside of the building, too as large as hundreds of thousands of dollars in missing merchandise. The extent of the damages can be wide-ranging.

So, who pays for these damages? Is the business owner responsible for the damages? Are the insurance providers responsible for covering claims related to protesting and looting damages? Or is someone else responsible? The answer is that it depends.

In most cases, the insurance providers will help out. If the automobiles of employees or private citizens were damaged, generally auto insurers will cover those damages after the customer pays his or her deductible. Standard homeowner's policies typically cover property damage due to riots. Most business owners also are required to carry insurance policies that cover damage to storefronts, business supplies, and merchandise. If the business owner does not have insurance, then he or she would need to cover the damage unless those responsible are found and can be ordered to repay for the damage.

In some states, there is also riot relief assistance available from the government. This is usually done through the state legislature and it is important to note that it is not an option in every state. In some cases, when no clear relief is available, community members have banded together to help sustain a small business without adequate insurance.

Chapter 23: The Need for White Allies to Join in Advocacy Efforts

It recent years, it has become apparent that to effect change people need to join together to advocate. It has also become increasingly important to align with allies who can help support the message. Since Blacks and other minorities have to experience systemic discrimination for centuries, it is White folks with privilege who need to speak up to help end racism and police brutality against Blacks.

Many people do not understand the role of White allies. Perhaps uninformed White people think that by sitting idly by and by not getting involved in protests, they are removed from the problem. However, the truth is that they are contributing to the problem since they are staying silent. What is needed now, more than ever before in history, is White allies who will stand up and advocate on behalf of Blacks and other minority communities who are continually being harmed by systems, like prisons, schools, and governments.

At this point, you might be wondering how you can become a strong ally? To become an Ally, you must first examine the role of your privilege. How have you benefitted from social and racial injustice? After you have examined your privilege, it is time to listen to what others need from allies. This involves listening to the needs of Blacks and other communities, it involves donating money and resources to organizations that support Black communities, it involves speaking up about microaggressions that you might hear, and it involves vulnerability. Part of being a good ally is speaking up whenever you see or hear about injustices. Becoming a good ally involves educating yourself.

The next step in being a supportive ally is to take action. Whether this means joining in protests that you believe in, helping to raise funds for a scholarship, or simply doing more to raise awareness of the oppression that exists in our society. Examine your talents and abilities to see how you can support the oppressed.

Chapter 24: Lack of Understanding of Looting by High-Level Government Officials

Throughout history, high-level government officials have handled looting and riots in drastically different ways. Recently, President Trump tweeted "when the looting starts, the shooting starts." He later sidestepped this tweet by claiming he was unaware of the racial undertones that this saying carried. Twitter took the unheard-of step of censoring the President's tweet in hopes of reducing the likelihood that his tweet would make violence seem like a viable option. When one explores the meaning behind Trump's tweet it becomes clear that the President would like to use strict measures to combat looting. This comment was made in response to looting and protests in Minneapolis after George Floyd was killed. The president intimated that he could send in supports, such as The National Guard to bring the city back under control.

Unlike President Trump, whose tweet brought on a swarm of backlash, Washington, D.C.'s mayor has been heralded for her response. Mayor Bowser has aligned with protesters in hopes of educating others. She had a huge "Black Lives Matter" message painted onto the road leading to the White House. She has worked with the police in Washington, D.C. to peacefully oversee protestors.

In China in 1989, students sought political reform for their country. However, the Chinese government responded with swift and harsh force. Using tanks, assault rifles, and other military equipment, they quickly brought an end to what had been a peaceful demonstration when they became killing demonstrators in Tiananmen Square.

Chapter 25: How does Police use Social Media to fight with Looters

As the previous chapter described, looting has been evident throughout history and across a wide variety of countries. However, looting is not as easy as it was in ancient times. Today, police forces across the world have developed more sophisticated tools to track looters and looted items.

Some companies, such as Apple, have sent out warnings to looters that their products can be used to track those who engage in looting. That is because Apple products have security features that enable the company to know when items were taken without being paid for. In those cases, a message will come up saying that the device is not able to be used and that authorities will be made aware of its location. Likewise, individual Apple owners can report their products as stolen and enact a tracking device that is embedded within the products to locate it. This is helpful because during the George Floyd protests one of the major targets for looters has been Apple stores.

However, not every item has tracking capabilities embedded within its products. So how do police contend with this problem while still working towards locating the missing items? They use a wide variety of techniques to track down and obtain missing items. One major way they do this is through the use of social media and other media mechanisms. Below are some ways that police can begin their search for missing items.

eBay

After looters steal something, they often have more than they can use for themselves or their families. Naturally, there is an instinct to want to sell the items to turn a profit. One of the largest online platforms for selling items is eBay. Police target sellers who are new or have an abundance of the missing items, such as having one hundred of the same pairs of sneakers for sale.

Craigslist

Another popular way to sell looted merchandise is to sell it on Craigslist. This website has much less scrutiny than eBay and does not require members to register. Thus, there is no record of how many items sold or what the sold items were. An additional benefit of Craigslist to looters is that many people buying the items can pay cash, so there is no electronic record. However, looters still have to list the item and picture of the items taken if they want to make the sale. This is where the police come in. If they are seeking looted items, they just have to find someone selling it. Craigslist is available across all fifty states so officials tend to look not only at one state but also in states close to where the looted items were taken.

To obtain them, police can pose as someone interested in purchasing the items during undercover operations. Postings tend to catch police eyes when there are a large number of the same items that are brand new with tags. Craigslist transactions have been known to turn violent in the past, so if you are considering buying something off of Craigslist make sure to do your due diligence and try to take safety precautions, such as meeting in daylight and public. Also, keep in mind that you want to avoid purchasing looted items so use your screening questions to learn more about the item you want to buy and how long the person has had it and where it came from.

Instagram

Instagram is an online platform that allows users to post pictures. Along with the pictures that are posted, users can post captions of the pictures as well. Instagram allows individual users to have followers. While there are some privacy options, many people fail to properly use these settings. As a result, police officials can look at users' Instagram photos. When people post photos of themselves looting, especially if their faces are not covered, then they can begin to track them down based on their profile information and digital footprint.

Facebook

Much like Instagram, Facebook also allows users to post photos. In addition to photos, people can create posts about what they are doing and write it out in text format. When people post photos of themselves or their friends looting, these photos are fair game for police officials to scour through. It often is not hard to figure out someone's identity based on their Facebook profile.

Television Footage

Although this is not exactly considered social media, the television stations play a major role in the apprehension of looters and stolen goods. That is because police can typically use footage taken during the looting and later examine it with the help of specially trained technicians. When the police identify even just one person, they can interrogate that person to find out who else was helping with the looting.

In general, social media provides a variety of ways to track down looters. Aside from the options mentioned above, if police have specific leads, they are also able to track social emails or messages that the suspect sent to his or her friends. In today's society which relies heavily on technology, police continually develop more refined methods to help apprehend those who engage in looting.

Chapter 26: What Do People Do with Stolen Goods and How Can Police Recover Them?

As described in the previous section, social media plays a large role in how people sell stolen goods as well as how police can intervene to recover stolen items. However, there is much more to the story of looting than just social media. This section discusses what looters can do with stolen goods and how police can recover them.

When people steal goods, they have a slight problem on their hands. They have to figure out how to use or sell the products, ideally without being caught by police. This sounds easier than it is. If looters are lucky enough to get away with goods, there is a strong chance that they could be caught later if they try to sell them.

In terms of selling goods, eBay and Craigslist are the two most popular sites that looters tend to sell items on. They can also sell stolen goods through neighborhood listservs. Another common way they aim to sell items is through informal networks, such as to family or friends of friends. This method tends to be the hardest for police to track. One other way people have tried to sell stolen goods is through pop up shops. After large instances of looting, police tend to scour neighborhoods to see whether any of these pop-up shops happen. When the coronavirus pandemic hit, some looters were selling masks, gloves, and hand sanitizer that they looted from hospitals for huge markups. Likewise, after looting during the George Floyd protests, some looters attempted to sell large quantities of sneakers and other stolen goods through these pop-up stands or shops as well.

Looters may also decide that the risk is simply too high to try to sell these items. They may end up using the looted goods for personal use or gifts, especially if the quantity is stolen was small and can't be traced.

For certain types of items, such as famous artwork or very high-value items, there is a black market that exists. Less is known about these illegal networks. However, officials from Italy, Greece, and other countries where the smuggling of looted artwork is more common do have techniques to find these items.
In many countries, in addition to the police force, customs officials play a crucial role in identifying looted goods that are coming into the country. As one example, a recent shipment of human hair to the United States from China was confiscated. It is thought that this hair came from prisoners who were subjected to human rights violations and therefore it was determined that this hair could not be bought or sold in the United States.

Customs officials have also used X-ray machines to identify items that could be looted. Thus, police have a variety of techniques, aside from social media, that they use to identify goods being sold illegally into the country. Police rely on detective work and tips from good Samaritans as other methods to track down looted goods.

Chapter 27: What Should I Do If I Want to Protest but I am Afraid of Looters?

When you feel strongly about a cause, it is natural to want to support that cause. Luckily, those located in the United States and many other countries around the world are encouraged and allowed to have freedom of expression. This includes joining a peaceful protest or rally in support of your ideological or political point of view. When deciding whether to join a protest, people think about whether or not it is safe. Seeing images of looting, destruction, and police brutality can make potential protestors feel that joining in a protest is unsafe. However, that is not always the case.

It is important to point out that the majority of protests are planned, peaceful protests where those in favor or opposition to a specific viewpoint are allowed to share their views collectively. In most cases, peaceful protests proceed as planned. However, in a minority of the cases, looting and violence can occur. Thus, it is important to think through how you can protect yourself and what to bring if you are going to join a protest.

You likely know about bringing the basic supplies. Never attend any rally or protest without water. While some places have water readily available, that is not always the case. Chances are that you will be outside in extreme temperatures. While some protests have First Aid centers set up you should not rely on these. Bringing your water ensures that you stay hydrated. Aside from that, if things get out of hand water can also be used to flush chemicals, such as pepper spray, out of your eyes, or to offer to a fellow protester who is feeling dehydrated. You can never have enough water.

Since police use recordings and surveillance to know who is attending protests and rallies, you should also consider covering your face with a scarf, bandana, or mask. Some people think this is only for those who are undocumented or who intend to cause problems. That simply is not the case. Covering your face makes using digital surveillance more challenging. Likewise, make sure to cover up any tattoos before heading out as well as to dress in clothing that is not distinguishable.

Aside from water, make sure you pack some healthy snacks to keep your energy up. Nuts or energy bars are good options. You may find places close to the protest that are open, but in some cases, businesses may be very busy or reluctant to serve those who are engaging in protests.

One thing that many people forget when heading to a protest is to take cash. Using a credit card will make it easy for authorities to know who attended protests and where they went. Using cash avoids this problem completely. Additionally, it lets you quickly get out of dodge if things begin to get dangerous. You can easily hail a cab, pay the bus fare, or simply give someone else some gas money to get you out of the area. When thinking about cash, it is important to think about where you will put it so it will not get stolen. Cash is useless if it falls out of your pocket while you are running. Consider putting your cash in different areas so that if some are taken or lost, you have some in a different place. For example, you could put some in an inside jacket pocket, some in a backpack or purse, and some on the inside tongue of your tennis shoes.

You may also want to consider bringing additional safety supplies, such as a flashlight, a small first aid kit, and any essential medications you need. Likewise, it is important to make sure that you have some form of identification on you in case you are stopped or injured. When thinking about safety, you will also want to make sure you have durable, closed-toed shoes that are easy for running in case you need to make a quick getaway should the protest get out of hand.

When thinking through other safety tips, one of them is to stick with the group you came with for the most part. You and your friends can look out for one another. However, if someone in your group begins to get violent or starts looting, it then becomes time for you to break away from that group so that you do not become endangered. Make sure you and your group have each other's contact information as well as a backup plan of where to meet in case you get separated.

When you are at the event, you will want to make sure that you maintain awareness of what is happening around you. That does not mean focusing only on what you and your friends are doing. You will want to know if someone close to you is instigating police, trying to break into businesses, or is displaying violent tendencies. If you see any of those things, you will want to move somewhere else or consider leaving. If the police decide to respond to any of those situations and you are close by, you could inadvertently become a target even though you were not doing anything wrong.

One thing that is important to think about is whether or not to take pictures. In some cases, the photos could be used to help track down people who engaged in illegal behavior. However, it could also be used to simply know who was at the protest and to keep tabs on innocent people. Thus, it is probably best to leave your camera at home.

If the police do decide to respond, you will want to get out of the area as quickly and safely as possible. This can occur when protests fail to disperse when they deviate from the planned path, and for many other reasons. To respond, police can use tear gas, pepper spray, rubber bullets, and other nonlethal techniques. If you notice as a gas-like spray, go in the other direction. If you get some on you, remember to use flush it out as soon as possible. Mill and lemon juice are helpful with pepper spray while waterworks to flush out tear gas. If you are hit with either one, you may need to also change clothing to get the smell out.

If you are stopped or arrested, you are not required to say much and it is generally in your best interest not to. You have the right to remain silent and, in most cases, you should exercise this right. Let the arresting officer know you would like a lawyer and ask to be allowed to use your phone call.

In general, most protests are safe and do not turn into looting frenzies. There are many safety precautions above that will help you plan how to safely attend protests and exercise your first amendment right. However, even if you are not the one causing disruptions or violence know that police can respond to others present who are. Thus, you will want to plan a getaway strategy and follow the safety tips outlined above.

Conclusion

Looting is nothing new and has been going on for centuries. In this book, you learned more about the definitions of looting and what constitutes looting. Interestingly, it also outlines why people loot, such as to obtain attention for their cause, out of a need to survive, and for other political reasons. One aspect of this book that may have been surprising is that there is no separate looting charge. Rather, people who engage in looting can be charged with a wide variety of other charges, such as theft, arson, and rioting, which can range in severity from misdemeanors to felony charges. This range of penalties makes it extremely important to advocate for good legal counsel if you or someone else is being investigated for looting. Thus, this book also helped you understand how to best handle the situation if you are charged with looting, such as retaining a lawyer and following his or her advice.

This book also outlines the differences between stealing and looting, which tend to be fairly similar to most people but different in the eyes of the law. Also discussed were which businesses are looted most frequently, such as those who hold high-value items or those that hold views in opposition to the protestors. It also explored arrest rates after lootings across different cities and countries.

Through this book, you also learned how police prepare for lootings, such as using riot gear, enlisting extra support, and making announcements to the public so people are aware of the protests and their potential impact. Also introduced in the book was which states and countries have the highest incidences of looting.

This book also explored two unique organizations that have been making huge strides in the fight for racial equality: Black Lives

Matter and Color of Change. Examples of each of their work were discussed, and options for becoming involved and donating to each organization were outlined.

One of the most important aspects of this book related to police brutality against Black people, such as famous cases where excessive force was used unjustly and what else can be done to prevent police brutality. In line with that, there were far too many examples that outline the huge epidemic of police killing unarmed Black people, such as in the cases of Tanisha Anderson, Breonna Taylor, and George Floyd. These cases are inextricably linked with recent protests and some subsequent looting that has occurred, as an increasing number of voices want to raise awareness that this is a huge systemic problem in American society.

As we turned from that topic to looting laws which were explored more in-depth. Additionally, this book reviewed tips for both business and homeowners so that they can protect themselves from looting when possible. Some ideas posited included using heavy-duty locks, having a guard dog, using security cameras, keeping pepper spray on hand, and considering the addition of steel bars to windows. Importantly, it also included thinking through safety plans in case individuals was at home or in the business during an attempt to loot.

One sizeable section that you read provided several worldwide examples of protests related to looting around the world. This included events in the United States, such as Hurricane Katrina as well as the Boston Tea Party. Additionally, it explored European events such as the archeological looting from Greece and the London Riots of August 6-11, 2011.

Towards the end of the book, information was provided about how looters see their actions. In some cases, looters know their actions are wrong and need the items to survive while in other cases looters can rationalize their actions based on some injustice they have experienced. It also explored the role that journalists play in maintaining and prosecuting looting.

A unique aspect of this book was a call that highlights the need for White allies to join in advocacy efforts for racial equality. Additionally, it discussed a lack of understanding of looting by government officials. A great deal of detail was discussed when exploring how the police are now able to use social media to combat looters, which is relatively new within the past couple of decades. As looting increases, so too does the technology and strategies used to combat it. Lastly, you learned about what looters do with stolen goods and what you can do if you want to attend a protest but wish to avoid looters.